WOMEN AND POLITICS
IN WESTERN EUROPE

WOMEN AND POLITICS IN WESTERN EUROPE

Edited by
SYLVIA BASHEVKIN

FRANK CASS

First published in 1985 in Great Britain by
FRANK CASS AND COMPANY LIMITED
Gainsborough House, Gainsborough Road,
London E11 1RS, England

and in the United States of America by
FRANK CASS AND COMPANY LIMITED
c/o Biblio Distribution Centre
81 Adams Drive, P.O. Box 327, Totowa, NJ 07511

Copyright © 1985 Frank Cass & Co. Ltd.

British Library Cataloguing in Publication Data

Women and politics in Western Europe.
1. Women in politics—Europe
I. Bashevkin, Sylvia
323.3'4'094   HQ1236.5.E/

ISBN 0-7146-3275-9

This group of studies first appeared in a Special Issue on 'Women and Politics in Western Europe' of *West European Politics*, Vol.8, No.4, published by Frank Cass & Co. Ltd.

All rights reserved. No part of this publication may be reproduced, stored in a retrieval system or transmitted in any form or by any means, electronic, mechanical, photocopying, recording or otherwise, without the prior permission of Frank Cass and Company Limited.

Printed in Great Britain by
John Wright & Sons (Printing) Ltd.
at The Stonebridge Press, Bristol

Contents

Notes on the Contributors		vii
Introduction	*Sylvia Bashevkin*	1
Struggling for Identity: The Women's Movement and the State in Western Europe	*Jane Jenson*	5
Feminism and Leftist Politics in Italy: The Case of UDI–PCI Relations	*Karen Beckwith*	19
Feminism and Religiosity: Female Electoral Behaviour in Western Europe	*Lawrence Mayer and Roland E. Smith*	38
Women, Politics and the French Socialist Government	*Wayne Northcutt and Jeffra Flaitz*	50
Party and Legislative Participation Among Scandinavian Women	*Ingunn Norderval*	71
Women's Legislative Participation in Western Europe	*Pippa Norris*	90

Notes on Contributors

Sylvia Bashevkin is Assistant Professor of Political Science at the University of Toronto. She is the author of *Toeing the Lines: Women and Party Politics in English Canada* (1985) and editor of *Canadian Political Behaviour* (1985). Her recent articles include 'Social Change and Political Partisanship: The Political Attitudes of Women in Quebec', published in *Comparative Political Studies* (1983) and 'Changing Patterns of Politicization and Partisanship among Women in France', published in *British Journal of Political Science* (1985).

Karen Beckwith is Assistant Professor of Political Science at the College of Wooster in Wooster, Ohio. She has done extensive research on women's electoral representation and policy issues in both Italy and the United States, and is the author of *American Women and Political Participation: The Impacts of Work, Generation, and Feminism* (1986) as well as numerous articles and conference papers.

Jeffra Flaitz is a University Fellow in the Department of Learning and Instruction at the State University of New York at Buffalo. She is co-author of 'Women and Politics in Contemporary France' (with Wayne Northcutt, 1983) and is preparing a dissertation on 'French Attitudes toward the Ideological Encumberedness of English as a *Lingua Franca*'.

Jane Jenson is Professor of Political Science at Carleton University and Research Associate at the Center for European Studies, Harvard University. In addition to numerous articles on Canadian and comparative politics, she is co-author of *Crisis, Challenge and Change* (with M. Janine Brodie, 1980), *Absent Mandate: The Politics of Discontent in Canada* (1984), and *The View from Inside: A French Communist Cell in Crisis* (with George Ross, 1984). Her contribution forms part of a larger study of the state and gender relations in France.

Lawrence Mayer is Professor of Political Science at Texas Tech University. He is the author of *Comparative Political Inquiry* (1972), principal author of *Politics in Industrial Societies* (1977), and co-author of *American Public Policy* (1982). He has published articles on party systems as well as the state of the comparative politics discipline.

Ingunn Norderval teaches political science at Møre and Romsdal Regional College in Molde, Norway, and is a Labour member of the Provincial Assembly of Møre and Romsdal. She has published a number of studies of politics in Norway and, as a further result of her practical political work, is writing a history of local Labour Party organisation in Molde.

Pippa Norris is Senior Lecturer in Government at Newcastle Polytechnic. She has contributed articles on gender politics to *Parliamentary Affairs, Social Policy*, and *Political Studies*, and is the author of *The Impact of Feminism* (1986).

Wayne Northcutt is an Associate Professor of History at Niagara University in Lewiston, New York. He is the author of *The French Socialist and Communist Party under the Fifth Republic, 1958–1981* (1985) as well as a number of articles on French political, social, and intellectual trends. Professor Northcutt is at present writing a political biography of François Mitterrand.

Roland Smith is Professor of Political Science at Texas Tech University. He is co-author of *Patterns of Recruitment* (1974) and has published several articles on American state government and politics.

Introduction

Sylvia Bashevkin

The modern women's movement has exerted a profound influence upon contemporary political thought, research, and action in Western Europe.[1] Despite important differences within – and cross-national in – the ideological and political orientations of modern feminism, the overall impact of this movement has been pronounced, albeit largely unrecognised and unexplored within the Western European and especially European politics fields.

The publication of this volume represents an important step towards bringing research on women and organised feminism, on the one hand, and European politics, on the other, to the attention of area specialists. Unlike many earlier studies, it goes beyond both the critique of conventional political research as well as the chronicling of modern feminism to analyse systematically the implications of the women's movement for contemporary European political discourse, public opinion, party activity, and governmental process.[2] To a large extent, then, these studies reflect a 'coming of age' of both feminism and women and politics research. It is hoped that they will contribute to greater research and teaching in what remains a relatively neglected area of European politics.

Aside from encouraging increased interest and awareness of this field, the purpose of the present volume is to demonstrate the wide range of theoretical and empirical concerns which inform ongoing research on European women and politics. Due to space limitations, the study cannot claim to be comprehensive in treating all European nations or all aspects of women and politics.[3] Nevertheless, it does identify common themes which point towards the political significance of recent changes in the social and economic status of West European women.

On a conceptual level, we open with a study by Jane Jenson of the challenge presented by the modern women's movement to the prevailing 'universe of political discourse' in Western Europe. By situating the origins of this movement in the European new left of the late 1960s and following, Jenson provides an historical context for her argument that the treatment of women by the state in Western Europe has altered substantially during the past two decades. In particular, she highlights the altered terms of address to women in France, where debates in the 1970s concerning abortion and contraception reform illustrated the ability of the modern women's movement to re-shape conventional (including older feminist) definitions of womanhood as maternity. Through a careful analysis of this process, Jenson argues that the women's movement has successfully challenged – but not necessarily transformed on a permanent basis – the treatment of females within the universe of political discourse in Western Europe.

The extent to which women have arrived on the European political agenda is examined with reference to Italy by Karen Beckwith. Using relations between the Italian Communist Party (PCI) and its former flanking organisation, the Union of Italian Women (UDI), as a focus, Beckwith questions how the universe of discourse in Italy generally and in the PCI specifically shifted during the post-war period. Rather than operating as a classic transmission belt for the PCI, a role which UDI fulfilled between 1945 and 1974, the organisation since 1974 has been challenged by the autonomous feminist movement to function as an independent political and financial unit. While Beckwith maintains that the universe of discourse in Italy and in the PCI has always been relatively open to the 'woman question', she shows that the altered treatment of women during the past decade has led, ironically, to the demise of UDI as the largest national women's political organisation in Italy.

In terms of its implications for European electoral behaviour, the women's movement has been assumed to promote, or possibly reinforce leftist partisanship among its activists and adherents. This hypothesis is tested by Lawrence Mayer and Roland E. Smith using quasi-longitudinal survey data from West Germany, Italy and the Netherlands. Their analysis indicates no significant relationship between gender and leftist party support, even among younger, university-educated and single women who could be expected to reflect feminist political influences. Gender was, however, found to be associated with religiosity such that in nations where organised religion had strong political salience, religious respondents (most of them female) tended to support non-left parties. These results suggest that assumptions regarding the attitudinal impact of contemporary European feminism are inconsistent with existing survey data on electoral choice in at least three European democracies.

The influence of feminism and women's changing political preferences is apparent in France, however. As documented by Wayne Northcutt and Jeffra Flaitz, women voted heavily for the left and especially the *Parti Socialiste* in 1981. Their support of the Mitterrand government, combined with a strong feminist presence within the PS, contributed to major policy initiatives on the part of a newly-created Ministry of Women's Rights. Under the direction of Yvette Roudy, this ministry aimed to improve the status of French women in the paid labour force, to increase access to contraception and abortion, to disseminate information about women's issues and to oppose sexism generally in order to enhance the power and autonomy of women. Northcutt and Flaitz argue that despite these efforts, as well as the recent gains made by women in élite-level political representation, the persistent economic crisis in France has taken priority in the minds of the female electorate and has contributed to a decline in the popularity of the Mitterrand government.

In terms of political involvement and substantive policy direction, the contemporary women's movement has also exerted considerable influence in Scandinavia. As analysed by Ingunn Norderval, the record of major Scandinavian parties in integrating women within the political system has been mixed, even though in comparative terms, women are quite well-represented among the political élites of Norway, Sweden, Denmark, Finland, and Iceland. Norderval maintains that only when women themselves began to pressure internally did the parties prove useful instruments for their political interests. She illustrates this argument through an examination of changes in female party support, the development of independent women's parties and separate party women's organisations, and efforts to improve individual female representation through numerical quotas and reform of the party nomination process. The article concludes that although feminists within the established Scandinavian parties face an uphill battle in their efforts to introduce procedural and substantive policy changes within these organisations, their withdrawal from mainstream party activity would lead to political isolation and a weakening of both the women's movement and prospects for democratic reform in Scandinavia.

Finally, obstacles to increased female representation in European legislative élites are addressed on a more general level by Pippa Norris. Using data on local, national and European parliamentary office, Norris tests the utility of three leading explanations of female under-representation. She finds that institutional (and especially electoral system) constraints rather than cultural or socio-economic barriers constitute the most important obstacle to women's legislative involvement. Cross-national differences in the political position of women are therefore unlikely to diminish without the implementation of electoral reform in majoritarian systems, even though the introduction of proportional arrangements within such systems remains doubtful.

Although each of these contributions emphasises different features of women's political status (or lack of it), all share a common view that the growth of the contemporary women's movement constitutes an important challenge to European political organisations and systems. While research by Mayer and Smith cautions against assuming the direct electoral impact of feminism in nations with a strong tradition of orthodox religiosity, these studies as a group suggest that the women's movement is an important influence upon political discourse, party activity, and public policy in Western Europe. In short, the willingness of European governments to address women as independent individuals, the growing numbers of female political élites, and the greater attention paid to policy issues of specific relevance to women together are evidence of the significant impact of modern feminism.

In addition, the articles included in this volume reflect a number of very serious dilemmas facing feminist women who seek to become active in mainstream (as opposed to independent women's) political parties. Beckwith identifies this problem as 'double-militancy'; that is, party women who are loyal to the anti-hierarchical and anti-patriarchal ideals of the women's movement, and who seek to remain active in that movement, must reconcile their feminist commitment with the often contradictory political demands associated with conventional partisanship. No easy answer to this tension emerges in the following pages, although studies by Beckwith and Norderval suggest that feminist partisans may face fewer dilemmas as they become more numerous within parties, yet at the same time retain women's movement reference groups either within or outside the same organisations. The problem which follows from disbanding such reference groups in favour of outright political integration is clearly illustrated in Northcutt and Flaitz's study of France, where the virtual institutionalisation of the women's movement within the PS following 1981 has left feminists dependent upon the electoral fortunes of an increasingly unpopular Socialist government.

The potential for retrograde movement on women's rights is thus implied in studies of France by Jenson and Northcutt and Flaitz, as well as in research on Scandinavia by Norderval. The possibility that anti-feminist pressure could roll back important gains made by the women's movement remains real, including in areas such as Scandinavia where cultural and institutional arrangements would appear at first glance to make political progress irreversible.

NOTES

1. I am very grateful to Brenda Samuels, Pat McAulay, and the secretarial staff at Erindale College for their preparation of the final manuscript.
2. Critiques of conventional political research include Judith Evans, 'Women in Politics: A Reappraisal', *Political Studies* 28:2 (1980), pp. 210–21; Thelma McCormack, 'Toward a Nonsexist Perspective on Social and Political Change', in Marcia Millman and Rosabeth Moss Kanter (eds.), *Another Voice* (New York: Anchor, 1975), pp. 1–33; Susan C. Bourque and Jean Grossholtz, 'Politics an Unnatural Practice: Political Science Looks at Female Participation', *Politics and Society* 4:2 (1974), pp. 225–66; and Murray Goot and Elizabeth Reid, *Women and Voting Studies: Mindless Matrons or Sexist Scientism?* (Beverly Hills: Sage, 1975).

    On the development of contemporary French feminism, for example, see Elaine Marks and Isabelle de Courtivron (eds.), *New French Feminisms* (Amherst, Mass.: University of Massachusetts Press, 1980); Maité Albistur and Daniel Armogathe, *Histoire du féminisme français* (Paris: Des Femmes, 1977), pp. 447–73; Jean Rabaut, *Histoire des féminismes français* (Paris: Stock, 1978), pp. 333–80; Annie de Pisan and Anne Tristan, *Histoire du MLF* (Paris: Calmann-Lévy, 1977); and Naty Garcia Guadilla, *Libération des femmes: le MLF* (Paris: PUF, 1981).
3. Recent studies which address nations not included in this volume include Monica Threlfall, 'Women and Political Participation', in Christopher Abel and Nissa Torrents (eds.), *Spain: Conditional Democracy* (London: Croom Helm, 1984), pp. 136–60; Edith Hoshina Altbach *et al.* (eds.), *German Feminism* (Albany, N.Y.: State University of New York Press, 1984); Donna S. Sanzone, 'Women in Politics: A Study of Political Leadership in the U.K., France and the Federal Republic of Germany', in Cynthia Fuchs Epstein and Rose Laub Coser (eds.), *Access to Power* (London: Allen & Unwin, 1981), pp. 37–51; and Helga Nowotny, 'Women in Public Life in Austria', in Epstein and Coser, pp. 147–56.

Struggling for Identity: The Women's Movement and the State in Western Europe

Jane Jenson

INTRODUCTION

During the first two post-war decades, politicians and social commentators in Western Europe complacently believed that older class conflicts over distributional questions had been laid to rest.[1] Welfare states across the continent organised varied programmes intended to protect their populations from poverty, disease and economic distress. These policies had been articulated by working-class parties and trade unions during the inter-war period and were often instituted by social democratic governments after the Second World War. Not only left-wing governments sponsored welfare state programmes, however, since virtually all post-war governing parties agreed on the necessity for basic redistributional policies.

In the light of this widespread consensus, many social theorists and political practitioners claimed that the 'end of ideology' had arrived. All parties were expected to turn from their narrow, class-based, protectionist positions towards a 'catch-all' strategy of cosseting capitalism in order to maintain economic growth. In turn, the fruits of continuing growth would be employed not only to protect working people from a repeat of the Great Depression, but also to provide them – and especially their children – with access to the opportunities which the new post-war era offered.

This consensus remained intact for approximately 20 years, until 1968 when student rebellion and resurgent class conflict marked the symbolic termination of post-war consensus. The years since 1968 have been years of crisis – both economic and political. The recent situation in Western Europe, then, has demonstrated the error of earlier assumptions about the end of ideology and, more importantly, about the soothing effects of the welfare state. Yet there has been no return to the *status quo ante*; rather, a new political situation seems to have emerged for which assumptions about pre-1945 politics provide little guidance. Perhaps the most novel feature of this post-1968 situation is the influence of what are commonly termed 'new social movements'. While there is widespread agreement among politicians and social commentators that these new movements are noteworthy, little consensus exists as to why they have become important, what their long-term consequences will be, or even what precisely they are.

This article focuses on one important new social movement, the contemporary women's movement, by examining its impact on politics in Western Europe during recent decades. While the discussion is clearly relevant to many – if not most – nations of Western Europe, the illustrative material is drawn from the French case primarily for reasons of space.

In this article, the women's movement is defined as a social movement whose actions resulted – either by design or by chance – in the emergence of a new collective identity. More specifically, this movement effected significant changes in women's condition and, in so doing, created a consciousness of the political salience of gender. It was in the name of the bearers of this new identity, women, that rights were demanded from the state. And, by promoting this new collective identity, the women's movement challenged both established analyses of social reality and established political practices by providing an alternate basis for female mobilisation.

DEFINING THE WOMEN'S MOVEMENT

A significant effect of the modern women's movement in Western Europe has been its modification of the parameters of the 'universe of political discourse'. By introducing into that universe a new discourse about women, the contemporary women's movement forged a new collective identity and utilised a discourse which emphasised the specificity of women's situation. It thus challenged existing assumptions about female identity. Moreover, because of its significant resource base and ability to shift the balance of political forces, the modern women's movement compelled the state to respond and thus differed clearly from earlier mobilisations of women, including late nineteenth- and early twentieth-century feminist movements in Western Europe.

Several implications for analysis follow from this definition of new social movements as originators of collective identities. First, it is important to specify the identity which the contemporary women's movement has formulated, and to differentiate this identity from those promoted at other times and by other social movements. Second, by defining new social movements in reference to collective identities, no *a priori* judgements are offered about the reasons for the development of the new movement.[2] Third, the research task thus defined is to account for the emergence and political impact of new movements.

What is novel about the contemporary women's movement? Bearing in mind the caveat that there is no single 'women's movement', nor any one place or organisation where it can be observed, it is possible to offer some generalisations about the range of positions which distinguish this movement. All mobilisations of women face two possible bases upon which to stake their claims: they may emphasise either gender equality or differences.[3] Twentieth-century arguments for the former stress the universality of citizenship in liberal democracy and claim for women the same rights to vote, work and participate in civil society as men. The identities which follow from equality claims are genderless categories of citizen or worker, which have frequently been sought by women in such mixed organisations as political parties and trade unions.

By way of contrast, feminists who emphasise gender differences focus upon those aspects of women's lives which differentiate them from those of men; this strategy has generally led to a consideration of the effects of biology and sexuality. There are multiple ways that this gender difference has been formulated, however. The first wave of feminism in Western

Europe, for example, made frequent use of maternity and women's responsibility for child-rearing as a line of gender demarcation. For these early feminists, women *were* maternal and claims for new rights and state policies were made in the name of mothers; the social identity thus underlined was that of mother and all women were expected to exhibit maternal behaviour.

Although many were themselves childless, early feminists assumed that women as a group would approach the world in a nurturing and selfless fashion, bringing maternal values to the harsh masculine sphere of politics. Claims for political rights – notably enfranchisement – were therefore justified as a way to inject female (i.e., maternal) values into politics. In this manner, as well, social programmes were designed not only *for* but also *by* women to promote the values of maternal feminism.

More recently, the contemporary European women's movement has also been motivated in large part by concepts of gender difference. It has not promoted a maternal identity, though, since the collective identity stressed is simply *woman* – an independent, autonomous female person with specific sexual characteristics but no automatic family status. The contemporary movement has thus adopted Simone de Beauvoir's label of 'other' and attached a value to it. Women are not to be devalued because they are *not* men. Rather, they are to be celebrated because they are women and, unlike the earlier identity, this category is not treated as coterminous with motherhood or maternity.

Rights demanded by the contemporary women's movement reflect a clear emphasis upon individual autonomy rather than traditional roles. For example, claims for unfettered control of fertility and reproduction, for the design of social programmes which acknowledge female independence from the family and men, and for societal and state action against sexism and marginalisation on the basis of gender all illustrate the independent identity championed by the modern women's movement. While this identity may have been invoked in earlier feminist mobilisations, it did not attain a hegemonic position in Western Europe until the late 1960s, when contemporary activists promoted it within what we will term 'the universe of political discourse'.[4]

POLITICAL DISCOURSE AND THE CAPITALIST STATE

The universe of political discourse defines politics, or establishes the parameters of political action, by limiting the following: first, the range of actors who are accorded the status of legitimate participant; second, the range of issues considered to be within the realm of meaningful political debate; third, the policy alternatives considered feasible for implementation; and fourth, the alliance strategies available for achieving change. The universe of discourse thus identifies those aspects of social relationships which are considered political, since among the multitude of tensions, differences and inequalities present in society only some are treated as political matters while others are designated as religious, economic or private questions. By defining politics, the universe of political discourse filters and delineates political activity of all kinds. Its major impact ultimately is to inhibit or, conversely, to encourage the formation of new collective identities.

This concept of the universe of political discourse may be viewed as a specification of some of the notions which Ernesto Laclau employs in his discussion of the 'impossibility of society'. Laclau posits a multitude of possible bases for the social construction of difference. In situations characterised by an 'excess of meaning', the production of meaning involves the imposition of a discourse of closure whereby from a number of possible paired differences (worker/owner, female/male, young/old, subject/other, mother/non-mother, etc.), some differences are embraced and others are ignored. According to Laclau,

> The social is not only the infinite play of differences. It is also the attempt to limit the play, to domesticate infinitude, to embrace it within the finitude of an order. But this order – or structure – no longer takes the form of an underlying essence of the social; rather, it is an attempt – by definition unstable and precarious – of acting over that 'social,' or *hegemonizing* it. ... Each social formation has its own forms of determination and relative autonomy, which are always instituted through a complex process of over-determination and therefore cannot be established *a priori*.[5]

This view of the social production of meaning focuses attention upon the material, political, and ideological parameters of discourse. Due to the relations of production in capitalist society, the universe of political discourse is unequally structured yet the specific identities which emerge from the social constitution of subjects cannot be known in advance.[6] Only an examination of each social formation and its discourse of closure can expose the struggles over collective identity which comprise much of its politics.

In the broadest terms, then, the universe of political discourse is a consequence of basic social arrangements. Changes in the mode of production create new occupational categories and alter the relations of production, making likely the emergence of new collective identities.[7] Similarly, societal religiosity and/or secularism shape the bases upon which collective identities can be built. For women, it is clear that post-war labour market needs for relatively inexpensive and often unskilled labour, as well as the expanded welfare state, are important factors underpinning the altered parameters of the universe of discourse – within which the contemporary women's movement has demanded reforms and created its own collective identity.

Basic social arrangements, however, provide only the limiting conditions for the delineation of the universe of political discourse; they merely facilitate, rather than guarantee, change in the prevailing discourse. Since the universe of political discourse is a political construct, it changes as a result of political struggle so that its character is also determined by ideological conflict. Social relations may be described in terms which encourage mobilisation around a new collective identity and a challenging set of policy demands, or they may be described in ways which discourage just such a critique.[8] New groups which attempt to introduce novel actors, issues and policy alternatives must therefore overcome the resistance of established political formations which act as guardians of the prevailing discourse.

The universe of political discourse, then, is the fence around the political which corrals some actors possessed of a legitimated collective identity and excludes others whose identities are thereby rendered invisible. For some social movements, recognition is no longer a problem, as illustrated in the case of European working-class organisations. Since the late nineteenth century, the universe of political discourse in Western Europe has accepted as legitimate both class conflict and worker mobilisation against capital, the capitalist system and the capitalist state. Similarly, peace movements based upon either cross-class or working-class alliances have long been recognisable within the prevailing universe of discourse. 'New' social movements, however, have been less intelligible and legitimate precisely because their concerns – at least until the late 1960s – were generally considered to be 'non-political' cultural or private matters beyond the conventional reach of social control. Only since the late 1960s have these movements succeeded in modifying the parameters of the political in order to place their concerns on the agenda.

The capitalist state has a major role to play in admitting or rejecting collective identities through its role in the interpellation of subjects. For example, the state helped to shape the identity of worker through laws and policies which incorporate labour into the wage relationship and provide a framework for that relationship.[9] The capital–labour relationship has varied across capitalist states, though, since some (primarily social democratic) governments have used state policy to promote a clear class identity, while others have addressed workers only as individual citizens.[10] Capitalist states have also varied across time and place in their contribution to the creation of gender, regional and ethnic identities.

Overall, then, the discourse of closure as mediated by the capitalist state establishes the potential for some types of collective identity at the same time as it excludes others. Moreover, the state frequently becomes the focus of collective struggle to gain legitimation for new identities and to alter the universe of political discourse in a manner which will allow new participants to translate their concerns into recognisable forms.

DEVELOPING A NEW COLLECTIVE IDENTITY

The successful emergence of a new political discourse about women in France since 1968 offers an important illustration of just such a change in the universe of political discourse. Struggles to alter reproductive policy in this period are particularly significant because it was in this realm that the contemporary French women's movement dramatically announced its arrival, demanded political recognition, and mobilised its constituency in a manner which rejected outright the prevailing definition of women on the basis of maternity. By pioneering a discourse which addressed women as subjects in their own right, the contemporary movement chose as its first target the French state, which had long appropriated for itself an explicit role in the social construction of gender relations.

Before 1970, the French state addressed women as either genderless producers who were seen as deserving the same economic and political rights as men, or as gender-defined maternal creatures who required separate and less than equal treatment. The former case is exemplified in the post-war Constitution of the Fourth Republic, which extended women's rights to work and to obtain equal pay. By way of contrast, the latter approach is apparent in post-war policy discussions of social insurance, family policy and reproduction, where legislators employed a discourse of gender difference – if not subordination. This second form of address approached women as inferior beings who held strictly familial and maternal roles; female identity was bounded by the familial realm, with obligations for child care (but not legal responsibility) and family stability assigned solely to women.[11]

This form of address was clearly reflected in the backward civil status of married women; until the mid-1960s, wives were legally minors, subordinate to husbands who could deny them the opportunity to pursue any activity or profession outside the home (including travel, job examinations, etc.) if such activities were deemed by husbands to be contrary to *l'intérêt de la famille*.[12] If the couple were married under a *régime de la communauté légale*, which encompassed about three-quarters of French couples, the husband had complete control over family resources and decisions because he was *chef de la communauté*. This inferior legal status of married women followed from the Napoleonic view of wives, entrenched in the Civil Code:

> *La femme est donnée à l'homme pour qu'elle fasse des enfants, elle est donc sa propriété, comme l'arbre à fruit est celle du jardinier.*

This status followed as well from the Roman-French legal notion of *offices viriles* (masculine responsibilities), which delegated men as the public representative of the family unit.[13]

This legal status was reflected in several post-war social programmes. Since family policy provided the foundation for the post-war welfare state in France, redistribution through family allowances was organised from those in society without children to those with many. This programme as implemented after the Second World War had the specific intent of shoring up the traditional family unit as an intermediary social institution between the individual and the state.[14] This Catholic-inspired view of the family assumed a hierarchical organisation with a male head; women's place was at home raising children and caring for the family. Family allowances to men and supplementary benefits for non-working wives all contributed to a situation in which the legal subordination of French wives was reinforced by social policy.

It was in the field of reproductive policy, however, that the state's form of address to women most directly reflected their inferior gender status. In restricting access to both contraception and abortion, the state subordinated the individual needs and choices of women to those of the nation – partly because the French state was profoundly concerned throughout the twentieth century about the implications for national well-being of a declining birth-rate. Military reversals in both world wars were attributed to France's low birth-rate.[15] State emphasis upon population growth was reflected in the infamous Law of 1920 which established severe penalties for anyone obtaining, providing or aiding abortions, and for anyone advocating the use of or providing contraceptive devices. This extremely restrictive law was further strengthened after the Second World War and remained intact until the mid-1960s.

From the perspective of the universe of discourse, it is important to note that the original 1920 discussion of abortion and contraception was conducted as if the provisions of this law had nothing to do with women. The legislation was debated solely within a discourse of patriotism, or the need of the French nation for large numbers of children to counter the prolific Germans. Analyses of population decline focused upon the financial hardships which large numbers of children imposed on families, as well as the moral degeneration of the working class which had produced a lack of responsibility in family matters.[16] Individuals guilty of contributing to depopulation were usually described as those men who preferred the easy life of the cabaret and café to that of *père de famille*. A system of medals and awards to fathers who rejected that lifestyle was established to encourage population growth.[17]

Inspired for the most part by visions of woman's maternal nature, feminists did not mobilise against the Law of 1920. 'Familial feminism' was by far the dominant stream in the movement between the wars; it was reflected in both Catholic and secular organisations, all of which used a discourse of gender difference and stressed the primary responsibility of women for safeguarding the family as well as the health and well-being of not only their children but also society as a whole.[18] French feminists, therefore, did not view control over their own reproductive capacities as a necessary part of their struggles, nor did they oppose state initiatives to protect and honour motherhood. They offered no resistance to the hegemonic form of address to women as mothers and proposed no alternative.

Opposition to the 1920 law and related pro-natalist programmes came only from the anarchist-led neomalthusian movement, which proposed a *grève des ventres* (womb strike) to block the production of children for a state which viewed them only as potential cannon-fodder and a cheap labour force.[19] The notion that 'wombs' and not 'women' were on strike provides striking evidence of the minimal attention paid to women's real-life contribution to reproduction.

This prevailing discourse of patriotism, which emphasised national needs, dominated reproductive policy discussions for many years. The only breach in the restrictive 1920 law and accompanying patriotic discourse was made during the 1950s by the Family Planning Movement, which lobbied for reform of provisions banning the use of contraceptives. *Planning Familial* (MFPF), however, challenged neither the discourse which claimed all reproductive capacities for state use, nor that which confined French women to an essentialist maternity.[20] Instead, the Family Planning Movement remained a movement for couples to gain control over their fertility and thus plan for their family needs.

The efforts of MFPF helped to ensure the passage in 1967 of *la loi*

Neuwirth, which established a very restrictive set of conditions under which contraceptive devices would become available. Debate over this bill in the National Assembly centred on the question of whether contraception was good or bad for families and the nation. *Planning Familial*, using this same discourse, argued that better families would result from controlled fertility. A legislative compromise made contraception an abnormal medical act, permissible under specific conditions which affected consumers, doctors, and pharmacists. First, contraceptives were made readily available only to married women and those whose age was not in question.[21] Second, since the law prohibited 'anti-natalist' propaganda, advertising and counselling about contraceptive use remained illegal.[22] Consequently, only couples who were already well-informed or willing to seek out information themselves were likely to understand the potential impact of regular contraceptive use. Despite *la loi Neuwirth*, then, *Planning Familial*'s effort to curtail illegal abortion as a popular form of contraception was not realised.

ALTERING THE UNIVERSE OF DISCOURSE

In many ways, *la loi Neuwirth* provided the last case of older forms of state address to women. A fundamental change in the universe of political discourse, including its treatment of women, occurred following 1968 and was clearly reflected in the campaign to reform French abortion legislation. The contemporary women's movement identified control over reproductive capacities as an early and primary focus of mobilisation. Given the resonance of this issue in the French population, the women's movement posed a major challenge to the state. In turn, it used this position to insist upon recognition by the state that relations of domination based upon gender did exist – thus making space within the universe of political discourse for a new identity for women. This struggle, however, has only altered the parameters of the universe; it did not fully discredit the prevailing discourse since abortion reform resulted from the articulation of several discourses and the equilibrium thus achieved was and remains unstable.

The women's movement appeared in France – as in most advanced capitalist societies – at the end of the 1960s. Women's situation was profoundly affected by both the rapid social change and the new political conditions of the post-war period. By the early 1970s, female participation in the paid labour force and post-secondary education had steadily increased for more than a decade. Rising divorce rates and urbanisation further challenged traditional family structures so that conventional forms of address to women rapidly lost credibility.

The political conditions of the New Left offered a beginning point for women's promotion of a new collective identity. In France, the New Left pioneered a political discourse which emphasised democracy and entertained the possibility that collective actors beyond the traditional working class could engage in revolutionary political action. Since an expansion of democracy in the workplace, in society and in political organisations was viewed as crucial to the creation of conditions conducive to socialist transformation, New Left politics provided women with the initial space necessary to claim their own democratic rights. They could organise around demands for new family relations, for political legitimation of gender-based difference and for acknowledgement that 'the personal is political'. Women's claims for increased control of their bodies and democratisation of family relations could be made along with demands for meaningful equality and democratic participation in work and social relations.

The women's movement also insisted, however, that because women faced specific disadvantages owing to their gender, they required political organisation without men and in an alliance of all women. Traditional Left goals of equal rights, derived from an assumed similarity between women and men, were thus replaced by attention to the specificity or distinctiveness of women's experiences. Only women could claim to have been systematically excluded from the public realm and forced to confine themselves to the private sphere. Only women faced directly the issue of reproduction. By homing in quickly on reproductive issues, the women's movement not only challenged older assumptions about 'feminine nature' but also excluded men – thus solidifying women's new collective identity.

By the late 1960s, a variety of groups and approaches with differing political roots had developed within what was increasingly identified as 'the women's movement'. These included radical, separatist feminists as well as activists who continued to work for change within established political parties and trade unions. Traditional women's groups were radicalised and new ones created.[23] The first major campaign in which many of these groups participated in France was the abortion reform movement, which emerged in large part from the unfinished business which remained from the 1967 *loi Neuwirth* and which was decidedly different from the Family Planning Movement.[24]

The campaign for abortion reform demanded change in the name of *women's* right to control their own fertility.[25] It was organised primarily by women-only groups and did not claim to be a campaign of professionals (even though it did accept the support of doctors who were willing to oppose the existing legislation publicly). The only criterion which united abortion reform activists was thus gender, and the discourse which flowed from their movement emphasised the liberation of all women – married or single, teenage or older, paid workers or housewives – and their right to decide for themselves whether or not to bear children. The question thus posed was less *when* (as it had been for *Planning Familial*) and more *whether* to bear children; within this revision, the rights of fathers and needs of the nation were clearly subordinated to the rights of women.

The strategy of the abortion campaign was also distinctive. It was designed not only to push aside taboos surrounding abortion and insist that 'personal' matters were truly 'political', but also to compel attention from the state by challenging its ability to exercise social control. Campaign activists recognised the role of the state in mediating and constituting collective identities, and thus deliberately engaged the state in conflict so as to further mobilise popular support for the women's movement.

The *Manifeste des 343*, published in 1971, was a public acknowledgement by 343 women prominent in French artistic, professional, intellectual and political circles that they had each undergone at least one abortion. This document, a collective confession of guilt under the Law of 1920, was followed in 1973 by a public letter from doctors who admitted having performed abortions. In this same period, the *Mouvement de Libération de l'Avortement et de la Contraception* (MLAC) organised well-publicised trips for pregnant women to countries where abortion was legal, and provided abortions in France using the Karman method.[26] Activists also employed more traditional political techniques including lobbying, mass demonstrations and public debates, alongside tactics designed to incite the state either to try to punish violators of the older law or to replace that legislation.

The French state did confront something of a crisis as a result. For many years, magistrates had warned that the Law of 1920 was not being enforced and that it was, in fact, unenforceable.[27] In addition, women were able to insert themselves into a volatile political situation in a manner which identified abortion as an issue of class as well as women's liberation. This was a serious problem for right-wing President Giscard d'Estaing, because the United Left candidate, François Mitterrand, was close on his heels in presidential electoral politics.

The case of the 1972 *procès de Bobigny* provides an excellent illustration of the strategy of engaging the state on its own terrain.[28] A teenage girl, along with her single mother and several of the mother's work colleagues who all held minimum wage jobs, were charged under the Law of 1920 after the girl obtained an abortion. The case seemed tailor-made for the women's movement, since famous and usually wealthy women who had admitted a similar crime in the *Manifeste des 343* remained free, while the state pressed charges against a poor unknown teenager, her mother (who had been abandoned by the father of her children when they were infants), and the mother's colleagues (who had acted in female solidarity). Both teenage parents in the Bobigny case were ignorant about contraception, since such information was available only to the already initiated, yet the boy could escape the predicament entirely. The girl's mother justified her actions as being what any 'good mother' who had failed to provide sufficient information about contraception must do.

Activists quickly adopted the case. The defence was argued by Gisèle Halimi, a founder of Choisir, but legal preparations were handled collectively by members of Choisir, other women's groups, and the defendants. Although the defendants gained a great deal of media attention and popular support because of the blatant inequities of enforcement of the 1920 law, little consensus emerged regarding the source of the inequity. For feminists, the case clearly involved gender inequality, as perpetrated by a state which employed women's reproductive capacities for patriotic purposes and for the promotion of traditional family arrangements. For other political actors, the case reflected class inequality, since the defendants were poor and thus could not escape from a law which did not punish the rich. For much of the legal community, the case represented a challenge to state authority which could best be resolved by a reformed and more enforceable law.

Each of these positions had some impact upon the *loi Veil*, which was enacted in 1974 because of unanimous support from left-wing opposition parties in the National Assembly. Given the plurality of motivations, then, the contemporary women's movement cannot be said to have dominated the universe of political discourse. The abortion campaign was successful, nevertheless, in expanding the parameters of political discourse in France. The challenge had created space for a new collective identity for women. By 1974, women's right to control their own bodies was one theme in the legislative debate surrounding the *loi Veil*, along with equity, fairness, and family planning.[29]

L'interruption volontaire de la grossesse (IVG, or voluntary termination of pregnancy) replaced *l'avortement* in official language. This shift meant that the state recognised women's choice in the very labelling of its institutions as Centres d'IVG. Further reform of the *loi Neuwirth* in 1974, which eliminated all age and procedural restrictions and permitted the advertisement of contraceptive products, was described by the Minister of Health as a simple process of normalisation to meet the needs of modern women.[30] Indeed, older concerns about the declining French birth-rate and its effects on the family which had dominated in 1967 were buried by the new discourse and the political forces supporting it. Finally, by 1981, state recognition of a 'women's' constituency reached a high point with the establishment of a well-funded and very visible Ministry of the Rights of Women, vastly expanded support for intellectual work by and about women, and increased state support to organisations of women.[31]

Of course, it was not only policies explicitly identified as directed towards women which changed; state policy in other realms began to demonstrate the effects of a new discourse. Labour policy was altered to train more women and girls; educational programmes reflected fewer traditional assumptions about the career path of girls; family policy changed to encourage mothers into the labour force as their children grew up, rather than making a supplementary payment for non-working wives.

The recognition of a new identity for women which the movement's skirmish with the state brought, also enhanced the ability of women to carry notions of women's liberation into other places in society. Political parties and trade unions, in some cases only after the success of the abortion campaign, reflected greater understanding of modern women's needs and promoted new positions.[32]

CONCLUSION

Such changes provide evidence that the contemporary women's movement did alter the universe of political discourse. They also illustrate, however, the precariousness of this process, since if the state has a role in establishing a discourse of closure, then it also holds an option to revoke what is 'given'. Allies of any social movement may remove themselves from the political coalition, and weakness may result. In addition, changes in the universe of discourse make that discourse available to enemies as well as allies, so that the former may extend the discourse in a negative direction. Opponents of Mitterrand's 1981 presidential candidacy, for example, employed the discourse associated with women and his support of the women's movement to launch a more general attack on Mitterrand, as the following campaign slogan indicates:

> *Il a avorté nos enfants.*
> *Il avortera la France.*[33]

Finally, because the production of meaning occurs within struggle over the discourse of closure, if social movements withdraw from combat they may return to their earlier condition of invisibility or older identities may gain sway. The contemporary women's movement succeeded only in promoting and, to some extent, legitimising a new collective identity. It did not oust the promoters of the older identities, who remain ready both to attribute social ills and crises to women and to agitate for a return to familiar discourses. Only vigilance can prevent a return to the patriotic and familial forms of address which, for so long, kept women and their words in the shadows.

NOTES

1. The project of which this paper is a partial report was supported by a research fellowship of the German Marshall Fund of the United States. This aid is gratefully acknowledged.
2. This position contrasts with those of Touraine, Gorz and other theorists of post-industrial society, who define the new social movements as manifestations of the exhaustion of social and political relationships in industrial societies. See A. Touraine, *The Voice and the Eye: An Analysis of Social Movements* (London: Cambridge University Press, 1981) and A. Gorz, *Adieux au prolétariat: Au-delà du socialisme* (Paris: Galilée, 1980).
3. This formulation is much influenced by Y. Ergas and J. Jenson, 'A Citizenship of Equality or Difference', unpublished paper, Center for European Studies, Harvard University, 1984. See also D. Leger, *Le Féminisme en France* (Paris: Sycomore, 1982), Part II, Chapter 1.
4. For details on several national cases see A. Coote and B. Campbell, *Sweet Freedom: The Struggle for Women's Liberation* (London: Picador, 1982); Y. Ergas, '1968–79 – Feminism and the Italian Party System: Women's Politics in a Decade of Turmoil', *Comparative Politics*, 14:3 (April 1982), pp. 253–79; N.G. Gaudillo, *Libération des femmes: le mlf* (Paris: PUF, 1981); and Leger, *Le Féminisme*, Part I.
5. E. Laclau, 'The Impossibility of Society', *Canadian Journal of Social and Political Theory*, 7:1–2 (1983), pp. 22–23.
6. For details of the unequal structure of representation in another setting, see R. Mahon, *The Politics of Industrial Restructuring: Canadian Textiles* (Toronto: University of Toronto Press, 1984).
7. By way of example, it is helpful to think about the process of mobilisation around a working-class collective identity. Such a collective identity provided a mobilising focus only after industrial capitalism was sufficiently advanced to make available a group of workers to whom that consciousness supplied meaning in their everyday lives.
8. Just as it is obvious that working-class movements can be mobilised only in industrial societies, it is also obvious that all industrial societies do not experience that mobilisation in the same way or to the same extent. Whether the organisation of the working class, *qua* class, occurs is a profoundly *political* outcome, dependent on the activities of political parties and other institutions of the labour movement. See M.J. Brodie and J. Jenson, *Crisis, Challenge and Change: Party and Class in Canada* (Toronto: Methuen, 1980); and I. Katznelson, *City Trenches: Urban Politics and the Patterning of Class in the US* (Chicago: University of Chicago Press, 1981). 'Exploitation', 'class struggle', and even 'the working class' are terms which take on popular meaning only *after* political struggle and *after* the hegemonic ideology has been breached by the worldviews propounded by organisations of workers. See A. Przeworski, 'Social Democracy as a Historical Phenomenon', *New Left*

Review, 122 (July–August 1980), pp. 42ff.
9. C. Offe, *Contradictions of the Welfare State* (London: Hutchison, 1984), pp. 108–9.
10. On social democratic cases, see G. Esping-Andersen, 'The Political Limits of Social Democracy: State Policy and Party Decomposition in Denmark and Sweden' in M. Zeitlin (ed.), *Classes, Class Conflict and the State* (Cambridge, MA.: Winthrop, 1980). On gender see J. Scott, 'Women in History: The Modern Period', *Past and Present* 101 (November 1983), pp. 141–55.
11. For a further discussion of the contradictory nature of this discourse and its utilisation by political actors outside of the state see J. Jenson, 'Liberation and New Rights for French Women', paper presented at Women and War Conference, Harvard University, January 1984.
12. For details see A. Michel and G. Texier, *La Condition de la Française d'aujourd'hui* (Paris: Gonthier, 1964), Vol. I, pp. 79–80.
13. K. Offen, 'Introduction: Aspects of the Woman Question during the Third Republic', *Third Republic/Troisième République*, 3–4, (Summer–Fall 1977), pp. 1–17.
14. There was, of course, a great deal of political controversy over this use of the family allowance programme. The left parties, especially the PCF, strongly objected to the Christian Democrats' insistence on separating family allowances from other social security programmes and organising them on a different footing. However, in the political battles of the liberation, the Christian Democrats won out and their formula was implemented. For details, see F. Goguel and M. Einaudi, *Christian Democracy in Italy and France* (Hamden, CT: Archon Books, 1969), Chapter 2.
15. For details see R. Tomlinson, 'The Politics of *Dénatalité* during the French Third Republic', King's College, Cambridge, 1983.
16. R. Talmy, *Histoire du mouvement familial en France (1896–1939)* (Paris: UNCAF, 1962), Vol. II, pp. 16–21.
17. H. Bouchardeau, *Pas d'histoire, les femmes* (Paris: Syros, 1977), pp. 119–20.
18. There was what might be termed an 'individualist feminist' current in the inter-war period, but it was very much in the minority. See K. Offen, 'Depopulation, Nationalism, and Feminism in Fin-de-Siècle France', *American Historical Review* (June 1984), p. 654. Bouchardeau, *Pas d'histoire*, p. 125, describes the lack of intervention.
19. F. Rosin, *La Grève des ventres: propagande néo-malthusienne et baisse de la natalité en France 19e–20e siècles* (Paris: Aubier-Montaigne, 1980), Part I.
20. Mouvement Français pour le Planning Familial [MFPF], *D'une révolte à une lutte: 25 ans d'histoire du planning familial* (Paris: Tierce, 1982), Chapters 6 and 7.
21. All products were sold only by prescription. Moreover, doctors and pharmacists were compelled to establish and guarantee the age and civil status of their patients by a system which required special prescription forms (more complicated even than those needed for drugs like morphine, etc.) for unemancipated (i.e., single) women between 18 and 21, and parental permission written on the prescription for girls under 18. See J. S. Cayla, 'Les Nouvelles dispositions législatives relatives à la régulation des naissances', *Revue Trimestrielle de Droit Sanitaire et Social,* 11 (1975), p. 2.
22. J. S. Cayla, 'La Loi du 28 décembre 1967 relative à la régulation des naissances', *Revue Trimestrielle de Droit Sanitaire et Social*, 4 (1968), p. 238.
23. For details of some of the groups, see M. Albistur and D. Armogathe, *Histoire du féminisme français* (Paris: Des femmes, 1977), Vol. II, Part IV, Chapter 4.
24. On the MFPF see Bouchardeau, *Pas d'histoire*, pp. 136–7 and B. Paillard, 'La Brèche féministe du planning familial', in N. Benoit *et al.*, *La Femme majeure* (Paris: Seuil, 1973), p. 97.
25. Leger, *Le Féminisme*, Chapter 2.
26. J. Mossuz-Lavau, 'Pouvoir de droite, pouvoir de gauche et problème de l'avortement en France (1973–1983)', paper presented at the European Consortium for Political Research, Salzburg, April 1984, p. 2.
27. D. Turpin, 'La Décision de libéraliser l'avortement en France', *Annales de la Faculté de Droit et de Science Politique (Clermont)*, 12 (1975), pp. 38–41.
28. For detailed discussions of this case see G. Halimi, *La Cause des femmes* (Paris: Livres de Poche, 1973), Chapter III and Turpin, 'La Décision'.
29. Mossuz-Lavau, 'Pouvoir', pp. 4–9.

30. Cayla, 'Les nouvelles dispositions', p. 3.
31. See Wayne Northcutt and Jeffra Flaitz, 'Women, Politics and the French Socialist Government', pp. 50–70 below.
32. J. Jenson, 'The "Problem" of Women', in M. Kesselman (ed.), *The French Workers' Movement* (London: Allen & Unwin, 1984).
33. This slogan is quoted by Pêcheux and Gaudet, who provide a fascinating linguistic analysis of the political reasons for breaking the grammatical rules in the use of this verb. M. Pêcheux and F. Gaudet, 'La Langue introuvable', *Canadian Journal of Social and Political Theory*, 7:1–2 (1983), p. 30.

Feminism and Leftist Politics in Italy: The Case of UDI–PCI Relations

Karen Beckwith

INTRODUCTION

The role of Palmiro Togliatti, General Secretary of the Italian Communist Party (PCI) from 1926 to 1964, in defending and expanding the rights of Italian women, illustrates the efforts of the PCI to involve them in the life of the post-war Republic and in the struggle for a democratic society.[1] In addition to its support for constitutional provisions which entrenched legal and economic equality, the PCI nominated and elected a relatively large number of female delegates to the Constituent Assembly[2] and organised female cells within the party structure.[3] The post-war history of the party is thus marked by sustained attention to the 'woman question', which Togliatti characterised as essential to the establishment of democracy following two decades of fascism.[4] In political terms, the PCI has recognised the importance of women's participation in and support for the party by creating flanking organisations, notably the Union of Italian Women (UDI).

In emphasising the importance of the 'woman question', however, the PCI has interpreted that issue in the light of its position as a Communist party which is committed to the primacy of the working class in effecting social change. The PCI approach is therefore grounded in partisan and not necessarily women's terms. Historically, the PCI has viewed women as a demographic group which must be organised, educated and brought into the party, rather than as a sector of society which shapes its own terms of mobilisation.

This dichotomy is clearly reflected in the treatment of women within PCI ideology. On the one hand, the PCI embraced women as workers in much the same way that it understood workers in general – that is, in terms of their relationship to capital, the means of production, the state and the party itself. In this sense, women were understood not as women *per se*, but rather as workers who happened to be female. On the other hand, the PCI also understood women as the wives and mothers of workers who provided stability and solidarity in working-class families. This second conception of women as crucial to family organisation was linked to the party's emphasis upon the importance of the family to workers. Notably, this second view did not address unpaid labour in the home, domestic violence, reproduction or other issues relevant to the familial relationship between women and men.

While PCI treatment of the 'woman question' therefore assumed the primacy of the party in the party–woman relationship at the same time as it understood women primarily in terms of their relationship to work or workers, the party has continued to stress the essential role of women in creating and defending democracy. For this reason, the 'woman question' has been a permanent and enduring issue for the party and, as a result, for Italy – such that post-war political discussion has been conducive to the inclusion of women's issues, concerns and needs. By emphasising female contributions to the wartime Resistance, the PCI employed its rhetoric and public actions to provide a political agenda which identified women as an important segment of Italian society. While the *content* of the discussion of women has varied throughout the post-war period, such a discussion has nevertheless been present.

In this article, we argue that the impact of organised women in Italy has depended primarily upon the potential for change in the electorate, the rise of other social movements, and tensions in the party system. In other words, the crucial factor for Italian women was not their struggle to be included on a national political agenda, but rather to find a way to determine the content of the consideration of women and to develop a politics appropriate to women and defined by them. Unlike the situation confronting them in many other nations, women in post-war Italy were considered from the outset to be an important and electorally crucial political category.

Frances Fox Piven and Richard Cloward (1979) suggest that the circumstances most conducive to the rise and success of social movements are the following: first, conflict among ruling élites which produces an absence of élite solidarity and hence possibilities which social movements may exploit; second, legitimation of goals of the social movement among some segment(s) of the élite; and third, change (or strong potential for change) in the electoral system which may create a shift in the balance of political power from one party or faction to another.[5] As Piven and Cloward observe,

> At times of rapid economic and social change political leaders are far less free either to ignore disturbances or to employ punitive measures. At such times, the relationship of political leaders to their constituents is likely to become uncertain. This unsettled state of political affairs makes the regime far more sensitive to disturbances, for it is not only more likely that previously uninvolved groups will be activated – the scope of the conflict will be widened, in Schattschneider's terminology – but that the scope of the conflict will be widened at a time when political alignments have already become unpredictable.[6]

In the terms of Jenson, above, we would suggest that the 'universe of political discourse' was already partially conducive to the presence and success of organised women in Italy. The 'actors who are accorded the status of legitimate participant' and the 'issues considered to be within the realm of meaningful political debate' have encompassed Italian women since 1945.[7] Indeed, the limitations upon organised Italian women resulted more directly from the limitations on 'policy alternatives considered feasible for implementation' and 'the alliance strategies available for achieving change'.[8]

This essay argues that post-war political changes affecting the Italian party system, the electoral balance and the relationships between parties and movements were conducive to the presence and success of organised women in Italy. It is not our purpose in this discussion to analyse all political movements in post-war, or even post-1969, Italy. Instead, what we seek to understand is how political conditions altered in such a manner as to affect one specific social movement, the women's movement, and how those changes shaped the relationship between the PCI and its main flanking organisation, UDI.

In examining this relationship we consider as first and foremost the more general linkage between women and the Italian left – specifically the PCI. This choice is felicitous for several reasons: first, the PCI remains the largest and most important leftist party in Italy; second, the PCI has devoted considerable theoretical attention to the 'woman question' as evidenced in the writings and speeches of Togliatti as well as newer PCI *Theses* approved at the XVth Party Conference in 1979; and third, the PCI played an instrumental role in founding the largest national women's organisation in Italy, UDI. In evaluating the presence and success of organised Italian women, we therefore focus in this discussion upon UDI, arguing that its eclipse by the mid-1980s resulted from changes in the universe of political discourse in Italy and, in particular, from the growth of an autonomous women's movement.

We begin by examining women within the universe of political discourse on the Italian left during two periods: the immediate post-war years until 1974 (the year of the national referendum on civil divorce), and from 1974 to 1984. Internal party changes and the pressure of a potentially changing electoral balance are addressed in this section. We then consider the rise of the contemporary feminist movement, the changing role of UDI, and the problem of 'double militancy' within UDI.[9]

WOMEN AND THE PCI, 1945-74

During the immediate post-war years, women were recognised for their important contributions to the liberation of Italy and to the Resistance movement. These roles were acknowledged in the granting of the franchise in 1945 not as a result of an organised, mass suffrage movement, but rather as part of an agreement between Palmiro Togliatti and Alcide De Gasperi. While it was widely recognised that women's votes were likely to benefit the DC disproportionately, both major parties campaigned for them in the 1946 elections; indeed, both the DC and PCI acknowledged women's electoral, social and cultural importance. Since the DC viewed women as crucial to family stability because of their roles as wives and mothers, it specifically organised women in flanking organisations and sought to address such issues as protection against divorce and wages for housework.[10]

While realistic about its limited chances of attracting the female vote, the PCI also viewed women as crucial to the existence of the post-war Republic. The party understood women's strength as centred in the home, notably in relationships with children and husbands, and feared the potential resurgence of fascism which could result from an uneducated female electorate. The PCI thus directed its organising and propaganda efforts toward creating female party cells and initiating UDI, which originally included women of all political inclinations, including Christian Democrats. The establishment in 1945 of the *Centro Italiano Femminile* (Italian Women's Centre, or CIF) by the DC, however, served to draw nearly all Catholic women out of UDI. For both parties, therefore, women were a distinct social group which was worth organising, attracting and representing. While each party had its separate but similar analysis of the 'woman question', the fact that 'woman' was identified as an important political category meant that the universe of political discourse included women from the very outset of the Republic.[11]

Given that the universe of political discourse was relatively open, the immediate post-war situation in Italy permitted the partisan organisation of women but not the growth of an autonomous women's movement, nor the rise of an explicitly feminist movement. The masses of women active in the Resistance were readily available for mobilisation, but the quickly 'frozen' party system combined with internal conflict within the PCI created political conditions unfavourable to women's political organisation other than through the two main parties.

This limitation on female political organisation is clearly illustrated by the case of UDI, which developed from the *Gruppi di difesa della donna* formed in 1943 to assist the anti-fascist guerrilla movement in Italy. Composed of, but not for, women, the groups provided strike support to the partisans and militated for political and economic change. Near the end of the war, some activists met to discuss the transformation of these war-based groups into a larger national women's organisation for peacetime, to include women who had been active in the *Gruppi femminili di assistenza ai combattenti della liberazione* (Women's Groups for Aid to Resistance Fighters), *Gruppi femminili antifascisti* (Anti-fascist Women's Groups), *Gruppi di difesa della donna*, and other anti-fascist women's groups. The motivating force behind the organisation of UDI as Italy's first national women's organisation was thus an understanding among parties of the left, especially the PCI, that the nascent democracy required support from women:

> Among the democratic parties of the left grew the conviction that, in order to proceed on the road of conquering democracy ... it was necessary to construct a mass women's organisation that could manage to join together, with a spirit of national and social solidarity, the theme of emancipation in strict connection with that of unity among the various political forces, and that would see the transformation of the conditions under which women live as part of the renewal of all of Italian society.[12]

The focus of the newly-established UDI was thus dual: it addressed both the role of women and women's issues as well as the establishment of democratic government in Italy.[13] While the PCI committed itself to these dual objectives, they were only temporarily endorsed by the DC.[14] UDI organised conferences about the problems of women and children, arranged for the movement of starving children from Naples to northern Italy, and sponsored cultural and recreational activities including cooking courses.[15] UDI also mobilised its members around such political issues as opposition to the *legge truffa* or 'swindle law' and monopolies, and support for the peace movement, agrarian reform and the nationalisation of energy resources.[16]

By way of contrast, issues of specific relevance to women but less important to the PCI remained undeveloped, so that UDI closely followed the policy lead of the PCI and did not demonstrate an independent analysis of such issues as women's status.

We therefore suggest that until the late 1960s, the 'transmission belt' model of relations between party and flanking organisation applied to the PCI and UDI.[17] UDI's political emphases followed the lead of the party and, with few exceptions, UDI followed rather than led even on issues of specific importance to women.[18] This situation developed for four main reasons. First, the demands of the post-liberation period, notably the construction of a democratic state, made nation-building and the elimination of fascism key issues which any national organisation, male or female, was likely to address. Second, UDI was financially dependent upon parties of the left, primarily the PCI, which transferred several million *lire* annually. Third, until its Tenth Congress in 1978, UDI had no rules prohibiting PCI leaders from holding leadership positions, so that those women who helped to implement PCI policy also tended to direct UDI policy. Fourth, most UDI members were (and still are) PCI members living in northern Italy, where fidelity to party policy remains strong. These last three factors permitted PCI penetration of UDI and, given the absence of a vibrant feminist movement to balance or challenge this influence, the pro-woman orientation of the organisation was clearly subordinate to its commitment to Italian democracy as defined by the PCI.

Developments in the Italian party system at this time further limited UDI options. The 1946 legislative elections were marked by the emergence of the DC as Italy's dominant party: the DC won 37.2 per cent of the seats, followed by the Socialists (PSI) and PCI who won 20.7 and 18.7 per cent respectively. The DC's strong showing in the 1946 Assembly elections has been attributed to women, who were expected to make the difference between DC and PCI electoral dominance. By 1948, the DC electoral position was confirmed and the possibilities for serious challenge from the PCI were eliminated when the Communists were completely shut out of government. While the distribution of Italian electoral results has fluctuated since that time, the party system and the arrangements of government have remained remarkably unchanged, with the DC retaining its electoral plurality and the PCI foreclosed from governing. The results of the 1948 legislative elections thus entrenched the basic post-war party system: the DC electorate was predominantly female, while the PCI had a disproportionately male constituency. Furthermore, the balance of parties was frozen with the DC in power and the PCI in opposition. As the political situation of the PCI became increasingly precarious, the political possibilities for organised women were limited.

Internal PCI tensions also affected women's political development. Galli and Prandi describe the goal of the PCI in 1945 and afterwards as establishing a new party, 'which, thanks to its organised presence in the country and in local governments and Parliament, could exercise leadership and push through reforms even though it represented the opposition'.[19] Since this goal met with less success than had been anticipated, the PCI faced criticism from within its ranks between 1951 and 1955 for 'having become a machine for the collection of membership cards, dues stamps, and signatures, a party without any political prospects'.[20] During this second phase, the PCI also faced problems in its response to international events, particularly the 1956 Hungarian revolt and Soviet reaction to it as well as the 'de-Stalinisation' programme within the USSR. Both of these events forced Communist parties generally to re-examine their goals and their attachment to the Soviet Union as a model of socialist revolution. While Galli and Prandi argue that the PCI held its own during the resultant 'third phase', it is unlikely that the party had sufficient ideological resources or incentives to examine the role of women at the same time.

The PCI was thus struggling internally, grappling with electoral politics and attempting to solidify its position in the party system so that it did not and could not develop a political climate favourable to either women's issues or a women-oriented UDI. Throughout the 1950s and 1960s, the PCI addressed few issues of specific importance to women and offered minimal policy initiatives on women's behalf. Neither active recruitment of women into the party leadership nor promotion of the few female notables within the party occurred; overall, both the number and proportion of PCI women in the Chamber of Deputies declined – a decrease *independent* of the party's overall electoral fortunes.[21] As well, UDI membership also declined throughout the 1950s and 1960s, although it stabilised by the 1970s as did female membership in the PCI. One explanation for decreasing UDI membership in the mid-1950s was

> a certain intolerance for the type of separate women's organisation [which UDI was], that was none other than the 'ghettoisation' of the women's movement in commissions and corresponding cells, separate from the party but not independent from it.[22]

By the late 1960s, external changes presented possibilities for internal reform within the PCI as well as for the rise of feminism in Italy. The 'economic miracle', the 'hot autumn' of 1969, liberalised divorce legislation, détente, and increased education and paid employment among women, provided the ground work for new social movements. The PCI under Enrico Berlinguer publicly declared a uniquely Italian identity (signifying its emergence as a 'Eurocommunist' party) and proposed a governing formula which involved both the PCI and DC (the *compromesso storico*). New social movements, particularly workers' and student movements, exploded the universe of political discourse in a manner which provoked internal change within the PCI and permitted the identification of what were previously viewed as 'lifestyle' or 'cultural' issues as matters of *political* debate. The PCI was thus forced to re-examine its relationships with flanking organisations and to reconsider its position *vis-à-vis* the working class. The results of this internal discussion included a reaffirmation by the PCI of its support for the workers' movement, recognition by the party of the need for labour movement autonomy from the party, and a restructuring of the PCI–CGIL (General Confederation of Italian Labour) organisational linkage.

The rise of 'new issues' and the transformation of PCI-movement relations did not immediately affect UDI, in part because the nature of party–movement ties remained unresolved throughout the 1970s and 1980s, and in part because the 'historic compromise' proposal complicated PCI treatment of the 'woman question'. The 1965 civil divorce bill, while not promoted as a women's issue, raised especially grave questions for PCI strategy. Since the Catholic Church and the DC strongly opposed any changes in divorce law, which they viewed as the exclusive domain of the Church, PCI support for divorce reform ensured no strategic benefits for the party. Indeed, since no evidence showed that the divorce bill enjoyed support among the masses of Italian women, PCI endorsement risked jeopardising the 'historic compromise', antagonising the DC and, at the same time, further alienating the female electorate.

None the less, the PCI ultimately and reluctantly supported civil divorce legislation in Parliament,[23] yet tried to circumvent a national referendum on the issue by helping to defeat the government in 1972. Such a referendum was inescapable, however, and the PCI waged a strong public campaign in support of civil divorce. This campaign offered an opportunity for the PCI to expand its popular base, especially among women, since the party had little to lose in its relationship with the DC by defending such issues as women's rights and freedom for women from unsatisfactory marital arrangements.[24] Newer, autonomous feminist collectives presented similar rationales, while the Republican (PRI) and Liberal Parties (PLI) argued their pro-divorce positions on the basis of freedom of choice. The PCI still relied upon old formulae in support of divorce; for example, one PCI poster showed four generations of women in profile with the legend: 'The family defends itself against fascism. The women of the Cervi family vote NO'.

Civil divorce was confirmed in the 1974 national referendum. From the post-war period until 1974, political conditions had largely foreclosed opportunities for the rise of an autonomous feminist movement in Italy and had limited the possibilities for UDI to focus more specifically or independently on the woman question. Although some exceptions do exist, the model of UDI as a flanking organisation and transmission belt for the PCI reflects the general pattern of PCI–UDI relations during the first three decades of the Italian Republic.

WOMEN AND THE PCI SINCE 1974

Within the PCI, a discussion of women's new role in Italian politics did not immediately follow from the events of 1969. The new workers' movement and its temporary alliance with the student movement during the 'hot autumn' of that year, however, forced the PCI to consider seriously its relationship to political and especially workers' movements. This reconsideration created a number of possibilities for the feminist movement since the legitimation by the PCI of the 'hot autumn' struggles provided encouragement and credibility for attacks upon and demands of the PCI. The rise of other social movements and the resultant instability inside the PCI helped to widen the universe of political discourse for women, as did a concomitant shift in the broader electoral balance.

The first evidence of a shift in electoral balance – and the shift's dependence upon women in particular – appeared in the 1974 divorce referendum where civil divorce legislation was confirmed by 59.3 per cent of Italian voters among an overall turnout level of 88.1 per cent. Two conclusions were drawn from these results: first, on 'social issues' such as divorce, the DC constituency was not as solid as had generally been held;[25] and, second, much of the support for civil divorce came from women who had long been considered to be traditional, clericalist voters and thus the core of the DC.[26] These results foreshadowed major political changes, particularly among female voters, which would eventually affect the electoral balance in Italy. Any decrease in female DC support would benefit the PCI and, in the 1975 administrative elections, the PCI indeed increased its share of the vote to 32 per cent and assumed or participated in government in 'just under 2500' towns and cities and six regional governments.[27]

By the time of the 1976 general elections, then, the PCI had cautiously recognised the importance of female voters.[28] This recognition came only gradually, and the party hesitated to take responsibility for the success of the divorce referendum.[29] However, as the electoral balance began to shift, and as women's votes became less predictable, the PCI began to make modest overtures to the female electorate and to the nascent feminist movement.[30] These overtures remained within the context of PCI dogma; that is, they were directed to the *movimento femminile* (women's movement) rather than to the *movimento femminista* (feminist movement).[31] The PCI in this period therefore engaged in limited, selective promotion of women to parliamentary seats, an effort reflected in the more than doubling of female PCI deputies between 1972 and 1976 (16 to 37) to a level which represented more female deputies than all other parties combined. This record was maintained but not improved in the 1979 and 1983 elections, just as promotion within the PCI party leadership remained limited. In 1979, the national *responsabile* for the PCI's Women's Commissions (Adriana Seroni) was elected to the nine-member party Secretariat, thus becoming the first and only woman to serve in this capacity.[32] Female representation on the Executive and Central Committees was similarly improved, although not to the same extent as legislative participation.[33]

In addition to its response to the women's movement on the level of numerical representation, the PCI also reflected interest in propaganda terms. In 1970, the PCI Women's Commission began publishing *Donne e politica*, a political journal devoted to the discussion and promotion of women's issues within the party. The main party organ, *L'Unità*, also gave increased attention to women's issues as did *Rinascita*, which frequently ran special sections devoted to this subject.[34]

Internal party discussion of the 'woman question' reached its peak at the XVth Party Congress in 1979, which was preceded by months of debate in party meetings and publications. The XVth Congress was devoted to the elaboration of PCI goals, policies and political perspectives, manifested in the writing of new party *Theses* which gave serious attention to the question of women and women's issues. Such questions as women's working conditions, employment opportunities, reproduction, child-care, male–female relationships, violence against women, PCI–feminist movement relations and female involvement in the party were addressed.[35] One of the most important sections, ('*Le alleanze della classe operaia*') concerns the PCI's

> ideal and political commitment for a relationship between men and women which leads toward a transcendence of the secular division of roles and is founded on parity; to ensure the conditions in which the will of women for liberation from all oppression can be fully expressed, including that which has been historically determined by sexuality.[36]

Formal party recognition that the 'woman question' is not completely comprehensible in terms of class conflict was reiterated as follows:

> it is necessary that a democratically organised women's movement be able to exercise, on a political level, all its power, and therefore have the strength to initiate not only economic and social changes, but also civil and cultural ones.[37]

Discussion of the 'feminist' portions of the *Theses* was quite heated, reflecting the crucial ideological challenge and shift implied by PCI recognition of specifically women's issues and, more importantly, the view that class struggle does not subsume struggle against patriarchy. Since the *Theses* acknowledge that oppression by sex is independent of class oppression, they represent the beginning of a modest change within the PCI. Before the discussion which led to the approved text, the PCI throughout its publications referred only to the *movimento femminile* rather than the *movimento femminista*. Its attempts to grapple with women's issues were coloured by a desire to incorporate women on the party's terms, so that the major 'women's issues' for the PCI had been how to assist the women's movement in creating an alliance with the workers' movement and how these social movements might work together towards democracy '*per uscire dalla crisi*' and '*rinnovare il paese*'. In the *Theses*, the PCI thus makes explicit its newly-found understanding of two key points: first, the need for social movements to remain independent of the party, and second, the party's willingness to support a 'third way' (*terza via*) towards such social transformation in Italy.

This proposed 'third way' combined with explicit acknowledgement that resolving workers' problems would not automatically resolve women's problems constituted notable changes for a party which had long supported women's issues solely from a working-class perspective. This modification, however, remains primarily a commitment on paper, since it is not at all certain that either the PCI leadership or membership understands the complex relationship between patriarchy and capitalism. And, while the PCI *Theses* address such issues as 'male–female relationships' (*un rapporto tra uomini e donne*), they also bemoan the fact that

> ... the problems of women, in their work, in motherhood, in male–female relationships, do not yet constitute, to the required degree, an integral and organic part of the programmatic platform and of the general political choices of the forces of democracy and the workers' movement.

The PCI commits itself to work in research for a solid alliance between the workers' movement and the women's and feminist movements. This alliance must find its grounding tension in order to get out of [the country's] crisis and reform society, and must search for its release in a society renovated profoundly, that has among its various characteristics a new condition of woman and a different relationship between women and men.[38]

In other words, the primacy of workers' struggles and of the transcendence of class society within PCI ideology remains paramount even in those sections of the *Theses* which are devoted to women's issues.[39]

UDI–PCI RELATIONS

The impact of the 'hot autumn' upon the relationship between the Italian trade union movement and the PCI ultimately affected UDI. By the mid-1970s, a movement–institution debate similar to that within the nascent Italian feminist movement was raging in UDI.[40] This debate manifested itself in discussions of the lack of autonomy of UDI, resulting from party domination of the UDI leadership, finances and organisational strategy. In particular, the PCI defined political activity in terms which were beneficial to itself as a mass-based, hierarchically organised political party. At UDI's Tenth and Eleventh National Congresses, efforts were made to revise leadership rules in order to exclude élites who simultaneously held other positions such as party or parliamentary office, so that UDI would develop a more independent stature. While this reform did not completely resolve the issue of double militancy at the leadership level, at the very least it offered evidence of UDI's efforts to regroup as an organisation committed to working on women's issues, rather than simply on general PCI-defined political issues of indirect relevance to women.[41]

At the Tenth Congress, too, UDI delegates voted for financial independence from all sources except members' own contributions.[42] Since the two major parties of the left had been contributing several million lire annually to UDI, funds to replace these grants would be raised by local UDI groups through local projects.[43] In addition to specific project-oriented fundraising, UDI locals would also fund themselves through membership dues, donations, subscription fees for *Noi donne* and *ND settimanale*, the sales of *mimose* (flowers symbolising the Resistance) and calendars, and UDI festivals.

The financial independence sought by UDI remained problematic despite these provisions. Since most of its membership was concentrated in the developed areas of northern Italy with a tradition of political activism, UDI activities in this region could be funded relatively easily. In southern Italy, however, UDI membership was limited and the organisation depended heavily upon contributions from the national PCI – which were difficult to replace and thus threatened to weaken UDI efforts in the south.[44]

In the north, too, replacing funds formerly provided to UDI by the PCI was not a simple task. In the summer of 1982, for example, UDI Bologna held a three-day *Festa dell'UDI* featuring book sales, food sales, games, toys and speakers. UDI Bologna netted approximately $150 on this event, a disappointing outcome considering that the smaller UDI Ferrara group had raised $200 in only one day by selling literature at the PCI-sponsored *Festa dell'Unità*.[45] While the financial advantages of organisational connections to the PCI were thus obvious, the Ferrara method of fund-raising contradicted the decision of the UDI Congress at the same time as it demonstrated the difficulties involved in trying to disengage from the PCI and its organisational resources. Moreover, the case of UDI Ferrara contrasted with UDI Bologna fund-raising illustrates the limited success of UDI in creating 'new forms of coming together' and 'a women's politics by women, for women'.

Lastly, UDI sought to transform its way of 'doing politics', as defined previously by the PCI, in the years after 1974. UDI was originally constituted in the hierarchical form most common to political parties and other male-dominated organisations; this structure became suspect and was eventually rejected (at least in part) as inappropriate to the needs and experiences of women, and as a source of PCI domination of UDI. Opposition to the PCI-dependent leadership of UDI was therefore linked to arguments for both policy and organisational autonomy, since it was agreed that the appropriate political *content* for women would not issue from UDI unless the group also assumed a more appropriate political *form*.

The movement–institution debate within UDI was also reflected in discussions of its relationship (as an institution) to the Italian feminist movement. While the traditional hierarchical organisation of UDI permitted it to relate more easily to the PCI, this same structure made interaction with the feminist movement more difficult. Hence, UDI faced two imperatives for organisational transformation: first, it required structural and political autonomy from the PCI; and second, it needed closer ties with the feminist movement in order to pursue the woman–specific nature of its original mandate.

We have already noted the extent to which the PCI began to recognise the importance of women's votes: by nominating women to Parliament and to a few positions of party leadership, by holding symposia on women's issues, and by discussing the 'woman question' at length in party publications. By increasingly recognising the 'woman question' as a crucial contemporary issue, the PCI also legitimised the feminist movement which, in this more supportive political climate, intensified its demands and brought increased pressure to bear upon the party. Therefore, while tensions between the DC and the PCI, internal contradictions within the PCI, and a shifting electoral balance served to expand the universe of political discourse, politics were continuously changing. The feminist movement exploited these tensions and contradictions, forcing new legitimations and new responses.

Pressures upon both the PCI and UDI to respond to women's issues were particularly strong in the period following the 1974 national divorce referendum. Majority support for divorce, in spite of a combined assault by the DC and the Catholic Church, marked a major change in the political orientation of Italian women and suggested promising improvements in female legal status.[46] Four years after the divorce referendum, access to abortion was made legal under liberalised, albeit limited, conditions; this legislation was upheld in a 1981 national referendum largely because of strong support and mobilisation on the part of feminist activists.[47] As early as the mid-1970s the autonomous feminist movement and the nascent Radical Party (PR) had begun to establish illegal abortion clinics in Italy, to organise 'abortion flights' to London, and to militate for changes in the existing abortion law.

The issue could not be ignored by 1975, when the PCI reluctantly broached parliamentary discussion of abortion reform following a decision by the Constitutional Court which declared unconstitutional an existing prohibition on therapeutic abortions.[48] The legislation enacted in 1978 struck out portions of the *Codice Rocco*, a fascist-era penal code, which defined abortion as a crime 'against the race' and thus prohibited the procedure entirely.[49] While the new law established some circumstances for legal abortion, it clearly did not provide full freedom of choice to women. Restrictions based on age and requirements which limited abortions to hospitals only following a physician's approval made the bill considerably less comprehensive than the feminist movement desired.

None the less, the bill passed the Chamber of Deputies in 1977 and was sent on to the Senate, where the constellation of party positions indicated passage by a narrow margin. To the shock and outrage of the feminist movement, the bill was defeated in the Senate, a defeat blamed on 'snipers' in the PCI delegation.

Although the Senate passed this bill only a few months later (in 1978) their original rejection of it provoked a massive debate among feminists concerning the relationship between their movement and the PCI – a debate which did not reflect well upon UDI. UDI had initially wavered on the abortion issue due to pressure from the PCI, whose working-class orientation could not easily assimilate or respond to issues which did not break down along class lines – especially when the item in question (abortion) threatened the PCI's flagging 'historic compromise' initiative. UDI's initial resistance to abortion reform provided yet another illustration of its ambiguity *vis-à-vis* feminism, and proved sufficient to confirm independent feminists' suspicions about UDI's subordination to the PCI.[50]

UDI thus faced severe criticism from the feminist movement concerning its adherence to a traditional nonfeminist, leftist analysis of women's role in Italian society, at the same time as it confronted internal pressures for reform. UDI's membership began declining in the 1950s, continued to drop throughout the 1960s, and stabilised only by the mid-1970s when it was believed that a change in policy was essential in order to attract new members and to maintain old ones. UDI activists became increasingly sensitive and later responsive to feminist criticisms of the PCI as a result; they began to reassess UDI's collective as well as their own individual roles in the feminist movement. In short, it appeared that UDI was no longer in the forefront on women's issues, but rather trailed behind a more militant, more articulate, and more attractive feminist movement.

At the Tenth Congress meetings in 1978, UDI members addressed the need for internal organisational change. They discussed developing *una politica per la donna della donna* (a way of doing politics for women by women), which would offer appropriate means of organising political action.[51] This change involved dismantling UDI's hierarchical structure and reorganising – in fact, rethinking – its leadership so as to offer increased opportunities for participation and decision-making by local UDI members and organisations, as well as better co-ordination of activities among UDI locals and with the feminist movement. At the same time, UDI needed to maintain a viable national organisation, group archives in Rome, and the *Noi donne* and *ND settimanale* publications. UDI's 'old' way of doing politics (following a male political form) was strongly criticised for permitting a few nationally prominent élites to make decisions and speak for all of UDI, and for directing local UDI organisations without sufficient understanding of the problems faced by women in particular regions or cities.

Changes within UDI were reflected in its joint efforts with the feminist movement to initiate legislation against sexual violence. In 1979, UDI, the *Movimento della liberazione della donna*,[52] the Women's Commissions of the PCI and the PSI, and autonomous feminist collectives in Rome gathered the 50,000 petition signatures necessary to propose legislation on sexual violence.[53] This petition drive was the first formal, nationwide project in which all Italian feminist groups – including those associated with political parties – participated. Its impact was clear, since by 1981 all of the main parties had proposed versions of a law on sexual violence.[54]

As in the case of abortion legislation, however, tensions existed between UDI and the feminist movement. UDI's role in the abortion issue had been to try to pacify feminists by convincing them to support a PCI-sponsored, more conservative version of the abortion proposal. According to some observers, UDI was too easily satisfied with this compromise abortion legislation, and did not sufficiently protest against its provisions permitting conscientious objection by doctors and restrictions on access to abortion for young women. Similarly, UDI's role in efforts to initiate legislation against sexual violence was also criticised as insufficiently militant.

THE ECLIPSE OF UDI

By the late 1970s, UDI faced two forces which threatened to restrict severely its political opportunities. First, the autonomous feminist movement successfully challenged UDI as the national voice of women; the former organised independently around *specifically* women's issues and offered a critical (at times scathing) analysis of UDI's relationship with the PCI. Second, the PCI was subjected to similar feminist criticisms which led it to open debate within the party on women's issues and to strengthen its standing among women – particularly young women – already in the party. In so doing, the PCI solved the problem of double militancy in part, since it created space for feminist women inside the party, and thus co-opted those who might otherwise have found another political 'home'. These two forces served to limit the political space within which UDI had traditionally operated.

As discussed above, UDI responded to change by attempting to institute new national leadership structures, a decentralised decision-making process, financial independence from the PCI, and autonomous local organisations. Efforts to implement these four internal objectives made it difficult for UDI to initiate meaningful political action or discussion outside the group's parameters; UDI was only able to respond (usually in negative terms) to the policy proposals of other groups. The inability of UDI to formulate a clear position on the issues of nuclear weaponry and peace, combined with its low level of activity on the sexual violence initiative, were cited by non-PCI feminists as evidence of the politically moribund state of the UDI organisation.[55]

UDI confronted three additional problems in this period. The first involved the fate of UDI functionaries (paid staff) who were to be replaced with local volunteer activists more familiar with local political needs and conditions. Rather than issuing from national headquarters in Rome to be implemented by paid functionaries, the new UDI political line(s) would issue from work circles in local UDI groups, and would be implemented by those local volunteers who were active, qualified and interested. The difficulty, however, was that many UDI staff members were mothers who had relinquished other, more traditional jobs in order to do political work for UDI at very low pay, and who found themselves unemployed as a result of internal organisational change. In addition, some way needed to be found of dismissing these functionaries without suggesting that they had performed poorly.

A second problem was that both ex-functionaries and local volunteers who replaced the paid functionaries became bogged down in routine administrative and fund-raising activities, at the expense of political work. In Bologna in 1982, for example, former functionaries recognised that a *Festa dell'UDI* was needed in order to raise money, decided to hold such a *festa*, and organised it with no protest from other members. One longtime UDI activist pointed out at a meeting, however, that because UDI Bologna no longer had paid functionaries, those volunteers who *were* active bore the burden of non-political administrative work and were distracted from more important political organising.

A third problem facing UDI was maintaining the support of older members, many of whom viewed post-1974 changes as self-destructive. While the opposition to change in UDI was complex, a serious generational conflict developed between the older (and sometimes founding) members of UDI, who revered the close PCI–UDI relationship, and younger, more feminist members, who saw UDI as a stagnant satellite of the same PCI which had resisted divorce and abortion reform. In a meeting called in Bologna to discuss changes proposed at the Tenth UDI Congress, one older member argued that the changes were a denial of UDI's past, a past that included strong ties to the working class. She argued that UDI was repudiating its historic commitment to progress not simply for women, but rather for the entire working class. She asked, 'Will we be advancing only ourselves? Are we denying our historic obligation to move others forward as well?' In fact, the resistance to changes proposed at the Tenth Congress was so strong in Bologna that another meeting had to be arranged to discuss the objections of older members, who boycotted the second meeting. In Reggio-Emilia, older UDI members were also so opposed to the proposed changes that they no longer attended meetings.

Any assessment of UDI's success in effecting internal reform and thus severing formal ties with the PCI must be made from the perspective of both UDI's own organisational viability and its broader position vis-à-vis the feminist movement. From the internal vantage point, UDI has enjoyed modest success. It has sustained itself financially and administratively so that the PCI and affiliated PCI Women's Commissions no longer control UDI as they did in the past. Externally though, UDI has been less successful. In political work on legislation against sexual violence, for example, the PCI Women's Commissions have been much more active in the last five years than UDI, although UDI may eventually be successful in organising around issues such as childbirth (*parto*) which are peripheral to PCI interests. Other issues may arise, like abortion, which the PCI considers taboo yet which a new independent UDI could pursue politically. However, it is not at all clear that UDI has been successful in increasing its external influence or in exerting political leadership on feminist issues.

In a peculiar way, this transformation of UDI may serve as a setback for feminism generally in Italy. The absence of the 'old' UDI means that the feminist movement lacks a constituent national organisation which has clear ties to the very same leftist parties that are most likely to be receptive to feminist initiatives. In other words, the 'non-UDI' component of the Italian feminist movement has neither a clear, formal relationship with the PCI, nor does it have a direct linkage with parliament – where 'women's issue' legislation is ultimately decided. The sexual violence proposal offers a test case in this regard.

It may be a reflection of perspicacity on the part of the PCI that the party welcomed UDI's attempt to develop *una politica per la donna della donna*. The idea that UDI might be fatally wedged betweeen the forces of a self-transforming PCI and the autonomous feminist movement was not a source of anxiety for the PCI or for its affiliated Women's Commissions.[56] While this process may simply have illustrated the working-out of the PCI's position on a *terza via*, it may also have been a recognition that UDI had lost its role in post-war Italian politics – a role now to be assumed by both the PCI and the autonomous feminist movement.

PCI responsiveness to women's issues, while more restrained than the feminist movement had hoped for or demanded, seems at first glance impressive but is less than surprising given that the universe of political discourse on the Italian left had never completely foreclosed discussion of the 'woman question'. The fluid electoral and broader political situation in Italy since 1969 – and, in particular reference to women, since 1974 – has thus offered an additional political incentive for change within the PCI. Ironically, these same conditions which have helped to create both a national, autonomous feminist movement as well as a more open and tolerant PCI position on the 'woman question' have also resulted in the demise of the Union of Italian Women.

NOTES

1. Parts of this paper were originally presented at the 1983 meetings of the American Political Science Association. I wish to thank Judith Adler Hellman and Stephen Hellman for comments and assistance on the revised essay. The PCI's defence of women's rights included commitment to civil and social parity between the sexes, protection of maternity and working mothers, equal pay, female enfranchisement and equal opportunity in employment. For a discussion of the drafting of the Italian Constitution, see Maryna Natoli, 'A trent'anni dal voto alle donne', *Donna e politica* 7:33 (April 1976), pp. 35–6.
2. The PCI elected nine women, or 8.9 per cent of its delegation (the overall representation of women was 3.8 per cent, or 21 women). For a comparison of the PCI record of nominating and electing women to national office with that of other Italian parties, see Karen Beckwith, 'Women and Parliamentary Politics in Italy, 1946–1979', in Howard R. Penniman (ed.), *Italy at the Polls, 1979: A Study of the Parliamentary Election* (Washington, D.C.: American Enterprise Institute, 1981), pp. 230–54.
3. See F. Cervellati *et al.*, *L'organizzazione partitica del PCI e della DC* (Bologna: Il Mulino, 1968); and Giorgio Galli and Alfonso Prandi, *Patterns of Political Participation in Italy* (New Haven: Yale University Press, 1970), p. 93.
4. The nearest English equivalent of 'questione femminile' is the awkward phrase 'woman question'.
5. Frances Fox Piven and Richard Cloward, *Poor People's Movements* (New York: Vintage, 1979), pp. 1–40.
6. Ibid., p. 28.
7. Jane Jenson, 'Women on the Agenda: Mobilization for Change in France', paper presented at the Conference of Europeanists, Washington DC., 1982, describes the 'universe of political discourse' as acting

    > to filter and define political activity of *all* kinds, designating it as a legitimate form, or illegitimate and even incomprehensible ... [A] crucial constraint on the activity and success of a social movement is the character of the universe of political discourse within which it must act. The existing ideologies ... severely limit the ways in which any social movement can have its concerns placed on the agenda. (p. 4).

    This concept is further refined in Jane Jenson, 'Struggling for Identity: The Women's Movement and the State in Western Europe' (pp. 5–18 above). The universe of political discourse therefore has an impact on the formation and content of political consciousness, collective identity, political action, policy options, and political movements. The concept 'universe of political discourse' is similar to Antonio Gramsci's concept of 'hegemony'. See, for example, Gramsci, 'The Formation of Intellectuals', in *The Modern Prince and Other Writings* (New York: International Publishers, 1972).
8. Jenson, 'Struggling for Identity'.
9. 'Double militancy', sometimes translated as 'double struggle', is the dilemma of an individual who is active in (usually) two sometimes conflicting political organisations or movements; in this case, double militancy refers to the conundrum of being both an active feminist and communist.
10. The DC established its female flanking organisation, *Centro Italiano Femminile* (Italian Women's Centre, or CIF), in 1945; women are organised internally in the DC's *Movimento femminile* (Women's Movement).
11. For English-language analyses of the PCI's perspective on women, see Judith Adler Hellman, 'The Italian Communists, the Women's Question, and the Challenge of Feminism', *Studies in Political Economy* 13 (1983), pp. 57–82; and Annarita Buttafuoco, 'Italy: The Feminist Challenge', in Carl Boggs and David Plotke (eds.), *The Politics of Eurocommunism* (Boston: South End Press, 1980), pp. 197–221. For treatment of the PCI and DC, see Karen Beckwith, 'Italian Women and Politics in the Postwar Period', paper presented at ECPR Annual Meetings, Freiburg, 1983, pp. 25–36.
12. Nadia Spano and Fiamma Camarlinghi, *La questione femminile nella politica del PCI* (Rome: Edizioni donne e politica, 1972), pp. 121–2. Translation from this and other sources by the author.
13. One of the first actions organised by UDI was support for the alternative of a republic in the

1945 national referendum; UDI issued a call to its members to vote in favour of the republic. See Giulietta Ascoli, 'L'UDI tra emancipazione e liberazione, 1943–1964', in *Problemi del socialismo* 17:4 (1976), p. 119.
14. For a discussion of DC support, see Spano and Camarlinghi, *La questione*, p. 123.
15. Ibid.
16. Ascoli, 'L'UDI', p. 139.
17. For description of the transmission belt model and its application to relations between the CGIL and the PCI, see Peter Weitz, 'The CGIL and the PCI: From Subordination to Independent Political Force', in Donald L. M. Blackmer and Sidney Tarrow (eds.), *Communism in Italy and France* (Princeton, N.J.: Princeton University Press, 1975), pp. 541–7.
18. It is worth cautioning, however, that a 'transmission belt' model can only be accurately applied to the case of UDI and the PCI if one examines the relationship from the point of view of the feminist movement. Ascoli, examining the UDI–PCI relationship in contrast to that of the *Union des femmes françaises*, argues that the Italian case is one of far greater autonomy, and that the UDI–PCI relationship has always been a subject of analysis and reflection on the part of UDI:

> The question of political autonomy from the parties [the PCI and the PSI] was posed by the women's association [UDI] since 1956, not as a result of the polemics under way in that dramatic and conclusive year between the Communist Party and the Socialist Party, but in relation to the analysis of the women's question, already considered as early as 1953. (Ascoli, 'L'UDI', p. 110).

19. Galli and Prandi, *Patterns*, p. 88.
20. Ibid.
21. See Beckwith, 'Women and Parliamentary Politics', Table 9–2, p. 243; and Karen Beckwith, 'Female Communist Deputies to the Italian Parliament: A Thirty-Year Retrospective', paper presented at Conference of Europeanists, Washington, D.C., 1979, pp. 3–4.
22. Maria Weber, *Il voto delle donne* (Milan: Biblioteca della libertà, 1977), p. 22.
23. See Beckwith, 'Representation in the Italian Parliament: Isomorphic Representation of Women and Policy Responsiveness to Women's Issues', paper presented at the Conference Group on Italian Politics Workshop, 1983, pp. 42–5; and Martin Clark, David Hine, and R. E. M. Irving, 'Divorce – Italian Style', *Parliamentary Affairs* 27:4 (Autumn, 1974), for two examples.
24. The modest reforms of the civil divorce bill included for the first time adultery by the husband as grounds for divorce; adultery by the wife had long been established as grounds.
25. On the outcome of the divorce referendum, Stephen Hellman writes:

> The obverse of the DC's humiliation was the vindication of the PCI. The importance of this cannot be overstated. For the first time since the 1946 referendum that abolished the monarchy, the PCI was clearly aligned with a majority of the country. And for the first time *ever* it was the largest party in the majority block ... The referendum seemed to open the floodgates.

Hellman, 'The Longest Campaign: Communist Party Strategy and the Elections of 1976', in Howard R. Penniman (ed.), *Italy at the Polls: The Parliamentary Elections of 1976* (Washington, D.C.: American Enterprise Institute, 1977), p. 170. Emphasis in original.
26. While men were less willing to eliminate civil divorce provisions than women, a majority of both opposed plans to restrict access. The following table shows the distribution of voter choice:

Voter Choice	Men %	Women %
Yes	35.1	45.3
No	64.9	54.7

See Giampaolo Fabris, *Il comportamento politico degli italiani* (Milan: Franco Angeli Editore, 1977), p. 57.
27. Douglas Wertman, however, claims that the female proportion of the DC vote stabilised at 60 per cent. See Wertman, 'The Christian Democrats: Masters of Survival', in Penniman, *Italy at the Polls, 1976*, Table 3–1, p. 75.

28. Stephen Hellman, 'The Longest Campaign'.
29. Stephen Hellman writes, 'It is significant that even in the midst of this dramatic turn in their fortunes, the Communists remained exceedingly cautious'. Ibid.
30. Maria Weber argues that by 1976, the women's vote was moving away from the DC towards the PCI. Weber, *Il voto*, pp. 28–31.
31. Judith Adler Hellman, 'The Italian Communists', passim.
32. The PCI Women's Commissions are the internal structure for the mobilisation and organisation of female party members. The status of the Women's Commissions has always been problematic, since they do not generally organise women around specifically feminist or women's issues, nor was this their intended purpose.
33. The following table, reprinted from Beckwith, 'Italian Women and Politics in the Postwar Period', pp. 53–4, indicates the percentage of women in the PCI leadership over time:

	1948	1951	1956	1960	1962	1966	1969	1972	1975	1983
Central Committee	5.6	2.3	8.2	7.8	7.1	6.6	8.1	9.7	13.0	14.0
Directorate	5.6	5.6	0	0	0	5.3	6.7	5.4	6.1	9.1

34. For examples, see *Rinascita* 4 May 1979 and 10 December 1982.
35. *Tesi approvate dal XV Congresso Nazionale del PCI* (Rome: 1979), *passim*.
36. Ibid., p. 675.
37. Ibid., p. 709.
38. Ibid., p. 712.
39. For an excellent discussion of the tensions between older, established party leaders and new, younger functionaries over the party's relationship to the feminist movement and the party's position on women's issues, see Stephen Hellman, 'Feminism and the Model of Militancy in an Italian Communist Federation (Turin): Challenges to the Old Style of Politics', in Mary Fainsod Katzenstein and Carol Mueller (eds.), *Changing Paradigms* (Philadelphia: Temple University Press, forthcoming).
40. For examples of the movement–institution debate, see M. Fraire *et al.*, 'Movimento e istituzioni', *donnawomanfemme* (*dwf*) 4 (July–September 1977), pp. 5–45; and response by Y. Ergas and M. R. Manieri, *dwf* 5 (October–December 1977), pp. 118–29.
41. A major problem in gaining autonomy from the PCI was the fact that a substantial proportion of UDI members are from Emilia-Romagna, a PCI stronghold, and many UDI members there are also PCI members. To prevent the domination of the UDI Congress by members from Emilia-Romagna, there was a specific *negative* quota for UDI members from the Red Belt; that is, UDI members from Emilia-Romagna were purposefully under-represented at the XIth UDI Congress.
42. Discussions about the possibility of financial independence from the 'father parties' (*partito pappà*) had already begun before the Xth UDI Congress.
43. Since the PCI and UDI have not made public the amount of money UDI receives from the PCI (and since much of the PCI's support comes in the form of contributions in kind), only estimates are possible.
44. According to UDI Bologna, UDI has 200,000 dues-paying members nationwide (based on national UDI data which may be inflated); between 35,000 and 40,000 members are in Emilia-Romagna, the region with the largest number of UDI members, 8,000 of whom are in Bologna. There are an estimated 12,000 UDI members in Reggio-Emilia.
45. Discussion at UDI Bologna, 14 July 1982.
46. For an analysis of the activities of the feminist movement around such issues as divorce and abortion, see Beckwith, 'Italian Women and Politics', pp. 7–25 and 'Representation in the Italian Parliament', pp. 42–62; and Yasmine Ergas, '1968–1979 – Feminism and the Italian Party System: Women's Politics in a Decade of Turmoil', *Comparative Politics* 14:3 (April 1982), pp. 253–79.
47. Ibid.
48. The PCI had introduced an abortion bill in 1972 and quickly withdrew it; the PSI deputy Loris Fortuna offered one in 1973; and in 1975 the PCI and PSDI introduced separate proposals.
49. On the abortion reform movement, see sources cited in note 44; Beckwith, 'Representa-

tion in the Italian Parliament', pp. 45–53, and Eleonore Eckmann, 'The Impact of the New Italian Women's Movement on Politics and Social Change', paper presented at ECPR meetings, Freiburg, 1983.
50. Feminists outside UDI claim that UDI followed PCI proposals on abortion, and that UDI endorsed the final PCI-supported version of the abortion bill, which had two glaring flaws: (1) the provision for 'conscientious objection' by doctors to performing abortions and (2) restriction of access to abortion for females under the age of 18. In addition, feminists claim that UDI was noticeably inactive during the 1981 abortion referendum campaign. However, in a general discussion at UDI-Bologna, UDI activists were emphatic in arguing that without the presence of UDI and the autonomous feminist movement, no abortion legislation would have been forthcoming – ever. For a discussion of feminist criticism of UDI in the 1970s, see Ascoli, 'L'UDI', p. 134.
51. In a meeting to discuss the changes proposed for the XIth UDI Congress in 1982, UDI members in Reggio-Emilia speculated about the possibility of looking to other groups or organisations, such as trade unions, for new models of organisation, and concluded that the kind of model which UDI sought did not currently exist elsewhere.
52. The *Movimento della liberazione della donna*, or Women's Liberation Movement, was originally associated with the Radical Party, and had helped construct the PR's parliamentary lists in 1976. The MLD split from the PR in 1978.
53. The Italian Constitution includes a legislative initiative provision requiring a minimum of 50,000 signatures. The coalition for sexual violence legislation acquired over 300,000 signatures from women.
54. For details of the sexual violence initiative, see Beckwith, 'Representation in the Italian Parliament', pp. 54–62.
55. It is interesting to note that UDI was 'unable' to make endorsements concerning proposals on nuclear weapons even though the PCI Women's Commissions established peace as one of their major organising issues.
56. See, for example, Silvia Neonato, 'UDI: separate ma senza rancore', *Rinascita* 47 (10 December, 1982), p. 19.

Feminism and Religiosity: Female Electoral Behaviour in Western Europe

Lawrence C. Mayer
Roland E. Smith

INTRODUCTION

A growing body of literature in the United States, much of which addresses the political impact of feminism and specifically a 'gender gap' in partisan attitudes, suggests that politically conscious women tend to vote for parties and candidates of the political left. This tendency directly contradicts the conventional wisdom in comparative electoral research, which maintains that women in general vote significantly more conservatively than men.[1] In the light of this difference, it is important to enquire whether a putative movement of women towards the political left in the United States is paralleled in other comparable, particularly Western European, nations. Our examination of this question should shed light on the extent to which feminist movements have developed and politically influenced democracies other than the American case.

The reasons why feminist movements could be expected to encourage women to vote for parties of the left are not difficult to discern. In most Western democracies, the principal opponents of the feminist movement have largely been the forces of the political and social right. The latter have generally resisted efforts to redefine traditional concepts of the family and within them, the 'proper' role of women. Feminist positions regarding contraception and abortion, which provide women with the opportunity to eschew conventional female roles, directly conflict with deep-seated values of the institutionalised right (e.g., orthodox churches). Since the traditional role patterns of men and women are defended by conservatives and widely opposed by feminists, the political interests of the latter would appear to rest in challenging the right-wing parties and political organisations which espouse the views of the social and religious right.

Of course, the identification of women with feminist goals varies across time and space, since women's beliefs are dependent upon such factors as religion. When religion is a salient identification for a person, we would hypothesise that it constitutes the most significant determinant of political attitudes, outweighing all other variables including feminist beliefs and socio-economic status. We expect, therefore, that religiosity constitutes an important intervening variable between gender and voting behaviour. Specifically, it follows from the above that people who are intensely committed to a conventional religion would be more likely to support conservative political parties than people for whom religion is not a salient force.

Are women more likely than men to be religious? On an impressionistic level, there would seem to be a relationship between gender and religiosity, emanating from the traditional domestic role patterns, limited education and lower levels of paid employment which conventionally characterise women as a group. Since orthodox churches generally support and legitimate the values associated with traditional gender norms, those women who adopt domestic roles could be expected to be both more religious and more politically conservative than non-housewives. This relationship is probably a reciprocal one, such that religious women may tend to seek or accept conventional domestic roles, while women in traditional roles may tend to be more religious.[2]

In addition, system-level factors may affect the relationship between gender and religiosity.[3] In those societies where religion is a relatively weak force, the linkage between gender and religiosity may be diminished or possibly eliminated. We would thus propose that if few people attend church regularly, then male and female attendance will not differ significantly. Overall, religion appears to be a more intrinsic attribute of the political culture – a system-level factor – in Western and especially southern European nations than in the Anglo-American democracies. In the former, church and state were not formally separated, permitting dominant religions to acquire an official or legal status, state financial support and extensive political influence. This phenomenon is clearly reflected in Italy (Roman Catholicism), West Germany (Catholicism and Lutheranism), and the Netherlands (Catholicism, Dutch Reformed Church, and Calvinism). As a result of the absence of church–state separation, we would expect religion in Western and particularly Southern Europe to be more politically salient, and more influential in the lives of its adherents (as measured by self-reported frequency of church attendance) than in Anglo-American cases.

Not only the degree, but also the type, of religious affiliation may shape political behaviour. Some religious denominations oppose changes in the role of women more than others. In particular, the Roman Catholic Church espouses a number of specific principles and values which conflict with feminist positions, as reflected in a 1931 encyclical from Pius IX (*Quadragesimo Anno*) which reads in part: 'Mothers have to work at home ... the fact that they ... are obliged to work outside their home ... represents an ... element of disorder, which has to be removed by any means'.[4] In contemporary terms, the church's vigorous stands against public access to contraception and legal abortion reflect its efforts to impose traditional child-rearing responsibilities upon all women, thus severely circumscribing their life and especially career choices. A serious commitment to Roman Catholicism, therefore, would probably prove incompatible with modern feminist beliefs. We would thus expect Catholic and similarly orthodox types of religiosity to encourage conservative political preferences, such that where women are significantly more committed than men to institutionalised religion (as measured by frequency of church attendance), they would tend as a group to be more politically conservative than men.

RESEARCH PROBLEM

In the following discussion, we examine the relationship between gender on the one hand, and party choice on the other. Party choice is defined in a dichotomous manner in our analysis; we distinguish only between parties of the left and those of the centre and right (also termed non-left). We hypothesise that in nations dominated by a salient orthodox religion, women will tend to be more religious (as measured by frequency of church attendance) and therefore more politically conservative (as measured by left/non-left party choice) than men. In such nations, religiosity will override gender as a determinant of party choice, since feminism will provide a weaker basis of self-identification than organised religion. Conversely, in nations where traditional religion is not a highly salient force, we would expect to find little or no statistical relationship between gender and conservative voting, and hypothesise that organised feminism has a greater chance of shaping women's views than in the former case.

Our reservations concerning the impact of gender upon party choice follow from three factors. First, women will vote as a bloc only to the extent that their gender (and specifically feminist) identification overrides religious, occupational, regional, ethnic or class affiliations, and only if gender is commonly perceived to entail specific policy or partisan beliefs. Despite media discussions of a gender gap in American political behaviour, therefore, it is unwise to assume that women vote as a bloc in Western democracies. As V.O. Key astutely observed in 1966:

> It is perilous to make inferences about what voters have or do not have in their minds from observations of the voting behavior of large groups of persons with like attributes: occupation, religion, residence, education. The inferences are most likely to be correct when the issues and the rhetoric of the campaign happen to affect directly and clearly persons of particular kinds ... Yet the fact that a person is, say, a Negro serves as an index to what he believes and to why he votes only when an election concerns Negroes as Negroes and when the members of the group are aware of the issue and see it as basic among their concerns of the moment.[5]

In this study, 'woman' could easily be substituted for 'Negro' in Key's statement.

Second, we would propose that gender has a weak influence upon political choice when other factors (especially religion, socio-economic class or party identification) override self-identification on the basis of gender, or when party competition is not perceived to reflect gender-salient issues. For gender to be politically meaningful in partisan terms, the programmes of some parties must clearly endorse feminist positions, while those of other parties must not.

Third, the absence of a statistically significant relationship between sex and party choice could follow from internal divisions among women concerning the implications of their vote. For example, women who believed that their interests would be best advanced through opposition to conventional role norms might endorse parties of the left, while others who sought to conserve traditional roles (the non- or anti-feminist vote) would be likely to support non-left parties. In other words, the elimination of gender-based classifications in the law might be opposed by women who sought to remain solely housewives and mothers, thus leading towards centre or rightist preferences. We hypothesise that the former group would be relatively affluent, well-educated, professional and tending to be heads of households compared with the latter group which, while led by well-educated and affluent women, might be generally composed of middle- and lower-class housewives who had less education than the first group. Age could also be a determinant of feminist leanings, since younger women would be more likely to challenge traditional concepts of a 'proper' female role.

This discussion suggests that there may not be a widespread consensus among women as a group on what are generally considered salient feminist issues, including equality in the labour force and broad public access to contraception and abortion.[6] We would note, however, that since women have been found to be more pacifist than men on policy questions related to military spending and the use of force, they may be most likely to behave as a bloc when political conflict centres on war and peace-related issues, and when electoral choices clearly reflect alternate perspectives on these issues.[7] Since the deployment in 1983 of American intermediate-range missiles on European soil, war and peace issues have become particularly prominent in Western Europe. The rise of the Green Party in West Germany is one manifestation of this phenomenon and, notably, much of its leadership has been female. Parties of the left have historically and in the contemporary period been more 'peace'-orientated in the sense of opposing military action and arms procurement in Europe and elsewhere. Given that the salience of these war/peace issues is growing, one might expect women as a group to show evidence of increasingly leftist political choices – the very same result which could be interpreted as a reflection of feminist influences. Even if women are increasingly preferring parties of the left, therefore, this tendency would not necessarily constitute direct evidence of feminist influence among women. Rather, it may also suggest the impact of war and peace considerations, which are themselves linked to broader feminist ideologies and activities in many systems.

DATA AND METHODOLOGY

In this study, the dependent variable of electoral choice is a dichotomous factor; responses were coded either left or non-left (the latter being centre and right choices combined). Our dichotomous treatment of the dependent variable permits greater comparability among the diverse party systems we are considering, namely West Germany, Italy and the Netherlands. In exploring the basic relationship between gender and electoral choice, we introduce a number of intervening variables: religiosity (shown by frequency of church attendance), religious preference, age, household status (head of household or not), education, occupation, subjective social class, employment status, marital status and, of course, party identification. Each of these factors is controlled in our analysis in order to elaborate the basic hypothesised relationship between gender and voting choice, using the 'elaboration model' discussed in Babbie (1979).[8] Both contingency tables and discriminant analysis are employed to determine which of the above factors best explain left/non-left vote.

Our data are drawn from West German, Italian and Dutch election studies, and from 1975 and 1983 Euro-barometer surveys which addressed the status of women in Europe.[9] These cases were selected for the following reasons: first, they have varying degrees of secularisation and religiosity, a variable which is crucial to our study; second, surveys are available from different points in time in each case, enabling us to examine longitudinal trends; and third, these particular data were readily accessible to the researchers.[10] We would note that the most recent election studies available are employed, but because the Dutch and Italian data extend only to the mid-1970s, it is possible that organised feminism has since produced a gender-based vote that is not evident in these data.

TABLE 1
RELATIONSHIP BETWEEN GENDER AND VOTING[a]

ELECTION STUDY	TAU-B	
Italy 1968	-.22	[b]
Italy 1972	-.09	[b]
Germany 1965	-.11	[b]
Germany 1969	.01	
Germany 1972	-.03	
Germany 1980	.04	
The Netherlands 1967	.00	
The Netherlands 1972	-.06	[c]

[a] Negative values indicate a tendency for women to vote for parties of the right. Positive values indicate a tendency for women to vote for parties of the left.
[b] $P < .001$
[c] $P < .05$

RESULTS

We found little evidence of even a moderate relationship between gender and party choice in these data, but did locate some support for women's greater tendency towards traditional religiosity. Overall, the strength of the relationship between sex and voting was related to the degree of female religiosity in each system. As reported in tau-b results in Table 1, the strongest tie between sex and voting can be found in the 1968 Italian data, where we identified a moderately strong relationship which declined by 1972 to a weaker but still statistically significant one.[11] Our German data revealed a relatively weak but statistically significant relationship in 1965, while the Dutch figures reflected a significant relationship between gender and voting only in 1972.

TABLE 2

CANONICAL CORRELATIONS FROM DISCRIMINANT ANALYSES OF THE RELATIONSHIP BETWEEN SELECTED CHARACTERISTICS OF VOTERS AND THEIR VOTE, BY COUNTRY AND YEAR[a]

GERMANY 1965 (87.8%)
Party Preference	.9437	Age	-.0924
Religiosity	-.1396	Social Class	-.0818
Education	-.0944	Marital Status	-.0804
Religion	-.0942	Household Head	.0777

GERMANY 1969 (93.4%)
Party Preference	.8636	Religiosity	-.1909
Religion	-.3175	Occupation	.1471
Gender	-.2716	Education	.1204
Employment Status	-.2353		

GERMANY 1972 (78.5%)
Party Preference	-.8385	Religion	.1933
Religiosity	.3105	Occupation	.0838
Education	.1960	Age	.0638

GERMANY 1980 (65.4%)
| Party Preference | .9978 | Gender | -.0883 |
| Eduation | -.1250 | Religion | -.0844 |

ITALY 1968 (88.9%)
Party Preference	.9921	Social Class	-.0409
Religiosity	-.0689	Household Head	.0335
Occupation	.0484		

ITALY 1972 (92.2%)
Party Preference	.9906	Social Class	-.0473
Religiosity	-.1235	Religion	.0458
Gender	.0951	Occupation	.0336

THE NETHERLANDS 1967 (81.7%)
| Party Preference | .8084 | Marital Status | .2487 |
| Education | .7285 | Social Class | -.2426 |

THE NETHERLANDS 1972 (93.4%)
| Party Preference | .9455 | Occupation | .1108 |
| Age | -.2571 | | |

[a] Figures in parentheses represent the percentage of cases correctly classified by the discriminant analysis. Since the dependent variable is a dichotomy, one would expect to achieve 50 per cent correct classification by chance alone.

As reported in Table 2, discriminant analysis indicated that gender did not function as a systematic predictor of the dependent variable. Rather, the strongest predictor of voting behaviour in all three cases was party identification, followed by religiosity, education and subjective social class. These four variables have also emerged as significant factors in earlier comparative electoral research.[12]

TABLE 3
RELATIONSHIP OF GENDER TO CHURCH ATTENDANCE AND OF CHURCH ATTENDANCE TO THE VOTE[a]

ELECTION STUDY	TAU-C GENDER	TAU-C VOTE
Italy 1968	.25 **	-.35 [b]
Italy 1972	.17 **	-.22 [b]
Germany 1965	.18 **	-.33 [b]
Germany 1969	.05 **	-.26 [b]
Germany 1972	.09 **	-.35 [b]
Germany 1980	.14 **	-.22 [b]
The Netherlands 1967	-.02	-.05 [b]
The Netherlands 1972	-.02	-.01

[a] Positive values indicate a tendency for women to say that they attend church regularly or for a left vote (both sexes) to be associated with regular church attendance.
[b] $P < .001$

As shown in Table 3, women tended to be more religious than men, as measured by tau-c relationships, to a moderate extent in Italy, to a lesser degree in West Germany, and not to a significant extent in the Netherlands. Clearly, then, system-level variation affects the relationship between gender and religiosity; we would propose that both Germany and Italy are characterised by fairly strong conservative churches where practising Catholics still, to a significant extent, vote their religion.[13] In the Netherlands, by way of contrast, the forces of secularisation have steadily eroded the electoral support of the three 'confessional parties' to the point where the latter have been forced to abandon their political independence and merged into a confessional bloc. In other words, Dutch Catholics, Calvinists and Reformed Church members are no longer inclined to vote their religion to the extent they once did but, rather, tend to vote on the basis of other factors, especially class.[14] Dutch confessional parties have thus sought to broaden their electoral appeal, nearly to the point of becoming non-ideological 'catch-all' parties.[15] Earlier levels of male and female religiosity in the Netherlands thus seem to have declined in the face of increasing geographical and occupational mobility.[16]

The data reported here therefore confirm our expectation that religiosity would outweigh the impact of gender on electoral choice. Even where religiosity is not a strong determinant of electoral choice – as in the Netherlands – other attributes including social class still override the gender factor.

TABLE 4

RELATIONSHIP BETWEEN GENDER AND RESPONSES TO QUESTIONS ABOUT RELATIONS BETWEEN THE SEXES AND ABOUT THE SPEED OF THE WOMEN'S MOVEMENT, 1975[a]

NATION	TAU-C RELATIONS	TAU-C SPEED
Germany	.16 [b]	.18 [b]
Italy	.11 [c]	.02
The Netherlands	.01	-.03

[a] Positive values indicate a tendency for women to say that relations between the sexes constitute an important problem and that the women's movement has not progressed quickly enough.
[b] $P < .05$
[c] $P < .001$

In longitudinal terms, we found a decline cross-culturally in the salience of religiosity in two of our three cases. Tau-c's for the relationship between religiosity and gender decreased from moderately strong to moderate in Italy; they also declined in Germany between 1965 and 1972, but revived somewhat in 1980. As noted above, this same relationship was virtually non-existent in the Netherlands in both 1967 and 1972. We would suggest that these shifts over time in both Italy and Germany may reflect the growing secularisation of both societies, although it should be noted that the most recent German data show a continuing significant strength in the relationship between religiosity and party choice.

This 1980 result obtains despite evidence from the 1975 Euro-barometer No. 3 Survey, which indicates a clearer distinction between men and women regarding feminist concerns in Germany than in the other two countries we considered (see Table 4). Notably, the perceived importance of relations between the sexes as an issue (on an 11-point scale) was greatest in Germany, next highest in Italy, and lowest in the Netherlands. A second question asked whether the women's movement was progressing 'too quickly', 'at the right pace', or 'not quickly enough', and again the greatest difference between men and women was in Germany, followed by Italy and then the Netherlands. Overall, German men were more likely to see the movement as proceeding too rapidly, while German women held the opposite view; in Italy, the attitudes of men and women were virtually the same; and in the Netherlands, men were slightly more likely than women to say that the movement was progressing too slowly.

In order for the feminist movement to produce a women's bloc vote, there must be not only a growing concern with feminist issues, but also clear gender differences in attitudes towards them. Only in Germany do we see such a gender difference, yet even in this case we are unable to identify anything resembling a feminist vote. That is, the tau-b for the relationship between gender and our dichotomised party choice variable was negative in 1965 and 1972, meaning that women were more likely to vote more for parties of the centre and right in those years. As well, we found little partisan evidence of female pacifism in the 1980 German data, since only very few (16) respondents in the sizeable sample (N = 954) voted for the Green Party, including five women.

The 1980 German data were also used in an elaboration model which considered the impact of age, education, marital status and household status on electoral choice. American research in this area has shown that being married is one of the strongest predictors of conservative political orientation among women;[17] hence, we would expect that female heads of household would vote more for parties of the left than other women. Furthermore, we predict that an 'ideal type' of woman who is most likely to hold feminist beliefs and to support parties of the left would be young, university-educated and a single head of household. Middle-aged and older women who terminated their formal education before university and who were financially dependent on their husbands are thus less likely to endorse feminist values and to vote for parties of the left.

TABLE 5

RELATIONSHIP BETWEEN VOTE AND CHARACTERISTICS ASSUMED TO BE RELATED TO SUPPORT FOR FEMINIST VALUES, GERMANY, 1980, WOMEN ONLY[a]

Characteristic	Tau-c
Head of household	−.01
Marital status	−.06
Social class	−.04
Employment status	.08
Education	−.02
Religion	−.14[b]
Church attendance	−.25[c]

[a] Positive values indicate a tendency for a vote for parties of the left to be associated with 'low' values on the independent variables (e.g., unmarried, not head of household, lower and working class, etc.)
[b] P < .05
[c] P < .001

Using the 1980 German dataset, we tested for a relationship among women between these demographic variables and our earlier religious preference and attendance factors, on the one hand, and electoral choice, on the other. Of all the independent variables considered, only religious preference and frequency of church attendance predicted voting choice to a statistically significant extent, the latter being clearly the strongest predictor (see Table 5). In short, none of the demographic attributes commonly associated with a feminist orientation was statistically related to voting for parties of the left. Hence, it cannot be said that these data support the expectation that by isolating those women who could be expected to hold feminist beliefs, a women's bloc vote would manifest itself. In addition, our German data show that women are not significantly different from men in their voting choices, a finding which contrasts with contemporary American research on a gender gap in party choice. Is this difference attributable to the differing feminist movements of Western European and American society, or possibly to a less clear distinction in the former between 'hawkish' and 'doveish' political parties and leaders? We would suggest that the development of a gender gap in European democracies – notably in the three cases we have focused upon here – may depend on the ascendancy of more clearly 'hawkish' leaders in major parties of the political right.

CONCLUSION

In this article, we have examined on an empirical level the implications of a growing literature on the political influence of contemporary feminism. Particularly in American studies of the 'gender gap', writers assume that feminism entails specific beliefs which, in political terms, translate into active support by women of the parties and candidates which best represent these beliefs. It is widely assumed that parties and candidates of the political left would thus be more favoured by women, and especially feminist women, than parties and candidates of the centre and right.

Our data fail to support this last assumption concerning the political impact of feminism in Western Europe. Using data from Italy, West Germany and the Netherlands, we found neither a tendency for women in general to be significantly more favourable towards parties of the left than men, nor a pattern for women with specific demographic attributes (including youth and university education) presumably predisposing them towards feminism to be more leftist than women with traditional backgrounds. Moreover, our analyses of Euro-barometer data did not support the view that women as a group are more likely than men to express feminist attitudes.

Rather, we found that the conventional wisdom identifying women as a conservative rather than liberal or radical political force was to some extent supported by our data. This relationship between gender and voting against parties of the left operated through the intervening variable of religiosity (as measured by frequency of religious attendance) and hence was qualified by the system-level variable of the salience of religion in each society. It would therefore appear from our study that where religion remains a strong social and political force among a large segment of the population, women as a group tend to be more religious than men – and since religious people are more likely to vote for non-leftist parties than secular people, we find that women are more likely to support the latter than men in such countries as Italy and West Germany.

Our results would seem to suggest that women in these three Western European nations are not a monolithic group in either feminist or partisan terms. That is, we found little evidence that men and women within nations differ attitudinally, a result which may be related to the relative newness of feminism as a political force, or to the absence of clearly distinguishable differences among parties on women's rights and war/peace concerns.

The data available to us thus indicate that conventional values, which are shaped and represented by traditional European religions, are a much more powerful determinant of voting behaviour in Italy, West Germany and Holland than feminist values. Not only do women generally not vote as a bloc, but also those who would seem to possess demographic attributes making them 'probable' feminists do not appear to vote as a bloc in these cases. Hence, the prospects for a women's vote in Western Europe do not seem encouraging in the short term. This of course does not rule out the possibility that such a vote might coalesce in the future as the strength of the feminist movement increases, and as the influence of traditional religion declines.

There is, however, a circular aspect to this problem, since to the extent that women appear *not* to behave as a feminist bloc in politics, politicians will feel less pressure to accommodate feminist concerns, particularly in the face of competing, non- or anti-feminist influences. And, to the extent that parties and candidates do not accommodate and reflect such feminist concerns, women's rights advocates will find it difficult to mobilise a cohesive voting bloc.

NOTES

1. See Joni Lovenduski and Jill Hills (eds.), *The Politics of the Second Electorate* (London: Routledge, 1981), p. 2.
2. See Janine Mossuz-Lavau and Mariette Sineau, 'France' in Lovenduski and Hills, p. 129, who report data from France that clearly indicate a strong relationship among women between religiosity and employment outside the home. Housewives, who presumably tend to be less educated than employed women, are distinctly more likely than employed women to be religious.
3. See Adam Przeworski and Henry Teune, *The Logic of Comparative Social Inquiry* (New York: Wiley, 1970), pp. 49ff.
4. As quoted in Maria Weber, 'Italy', in Lovenduski and Hills, p. 185.
5. V.O. Key, *The Responsible Electorate* (Cambridge: Harvard University Press, 1966), p. 70.
6. See Virginia Sapiro, *The Political Integration of Women* (Urbana: University of Illinois Press, 1983), pp. 143–69 for further discussion of this conflict among women.
7. See Sandra Baxter and Marjorie Lansing, *Women and Politics* (Ann Arbor: University of Michigan Press, 1983), pp. 58–59.
8. Earl Babbie, *The Practice of Social Research* (Belmont, CA: Wadsworth, 1979), pp. 445–69.
9. Surveys employed were the following: Divo-institut fuer Wirtschaftsforschung, October 1965 German Election Study; Felix Heunks, M. Kent Jennings, Warren E. Miller, Philip C. Southard and Jacques Thomassen, Dutch Election Study, 1970–73; Samuel Barnes, Italian Mass Election Survey, 1968; Samuel Barnes and Giacomo Sani, Italian Mass Election Survey, 1972; Manfred Berger, Wolfgang Gibowski, Max Kaase, Dieter Roth, Uwe Schleth and Rudolf Wildenmann, 1972 German Election Panel Study; Max Kaase, Uwe Schleth, Wolfgang Adrain, Manfred Berger and Rudolf Wildenmann, August and September 1969 German Election Study; Jacques-René Rabier and Ronald Inglehart, Euro-barometer No. 3 (May 1975); and Jacques-René Rabier, Hélène Riffault and Ronald Inglehart, Euro-barometer No. 19 (April 1983). All were made available through the Inter-University Consortium for Political and Social Research. Neither the original investigators

nor the ICPSR bears responsibility for the analyses or interpretations presented here.
10. For an analysis of these same sources as well as the 1980 American National Election Study, see Lawrence C. Mayer and Roland E. Smith, 'The Impact of Gender on Electoral Choice in Western Democracies', paper presented to American Political Science Association meetings, Chicago, 1983.
11. Tau-b and tau-c were used as measures of association in order to compare among a number of symmetrical and assymmetrical contingency tables. Tau tends to be of lower magnitude than gamma but it has the advantage of providing for a large number of ties. Phi is only appropriate for 2 × 2 tables, while gamma does not make allowance for either ties or table size. See Norman H. Nie (*et al.*), *SPSS: Statistical Package for the Social Sciences* (New York: McGraw-Hill, 1975), pp. 224–8.
12. See Philip E. Converse, 'Religion and Politics: The 1960 Election', in Angus Campbell *et al.*, *Elections and the Political Order* (New York: Wiley, 1966), pp. 96–124.
13. See David B. Conradt, *The German Polity* (New York: Longman, 1982), p. 130; Rafael Zariski, *Italy* (Hinsdale: Dryden, 1972), pp. 171ff.
14. See Steven Wolinetz, 'Electoral Change and Attempts to Build Catch-all Parties in the Netherlands', paper presented to Canadian Political Science Association meetings, Montreal, 1973.
15. See Otto Kirchheimer, 'The Transformation of Western European Party Systems', in Joseph LaPalombara and Myron Weiner (eds.), *Political Parties and Political Development* (Princeton: Princeton University Press, 1966), pp. 177–200; and Lawrence Mayer with John Burnett, *Politics in Industrial Societies* (New York: Wiley, 1977), p. 276.
16. See Herman Bakvis, *Catholic Power in the Netherlands* (Montreal: McGill-Queen's University Press, 1981), p. 155.
17. See Sapiro, *Political Integration*, pp. 151–3.

Women, Politics and the French Socialist Government

Wayne Northcutt
Jeffra Flaitz

In contemporary France, as in other European and North American countries, politicians are demonstrating increased interest in the votes of women.[1] François Mitterrand, for example, has frequently stated that he would have become President in both 1965 and 1974 had he captured the political support of French women. Since their formal enfranchisement in 1944, the female electorate of France – approximately 53 per cent of the voting population – has manifested a gradual shift to the left. In 1981, this trend among women contributed significantly to a *phénomène socialiste* which ushered into power Mitterrand and his *Parti socialiste* (PS).[2]

Despite the efforts of both Mitterrand and the newly created Ministry of Women's Rights to improve the condition of women, however, the female electorate now appears to be undergoing a *recentrage*, or a retreat away from the left. In order to understand better this series of changes in women's political allegiances, it is important to examine closely their attitudes and political choices before 1981, the reasons why women voted for the Socialists in 1981, and the subsequent record of the Mitterrand government (including the work of the Ministry of Women's Rights). This article maintains that women's changing preferences both before and after 1981 are related to a number of wider political, economic, and social factors, which also shape the broader fortunes of Mitterrand's Socialist government.

POLITICAL PREFERENCES 1944–81

Among the most intriguing aspects of post-war French politics is the increased politicisation and leftism of women voters. As outlined in Bashevkin (1985), de Gaulle extended the franchise to women in 1944, partly because of the important role which many had played in the Resistance and partly because he required female support in order to construct a revitalised republic after the war. Overall, leftist parties tended to favour enfranchisement on ideological grounds, but feared its electoral consequences, while the Catholic Church opposed changes in the status of women but realised that enfranchisement might aid conservative political interests.[3] Indeed, women's inexperience with the levers of political power, the strong influence of the church and the fact that de Gaulle granted them the vote seemed to foster conservative voting patterns among women in the years following 1944.

A number of factors have since helped to transform the political behaviour of French women. The rapid pace of post-war urbanisation, industrialisation and secularisation, which exposed women to a greater variety of political parties, was followed by the rise of the new left and the student–worker revolt of 1968, which provided the backdrop for a rebirth of organised French feminism. These developments, accompanied by growing access among women to higher education and employment opportunities, and by a willingness on the part of leftist parties to mobilise women, worked to politicise the female electorate in a distinctively leftist direction.[4]

Empirical research demonstrates that from the early post-war years to the late 1970s, French women displayed increased political interest, diminished levels of electoral abstention and greater willingness to identify with a political party – all important indicators of growing politicisation. In 1953, for example, only 40 per cent of female voters stated that they were interested in politics compared with 72 per cent of male voters, while by 1978 women's interest in politics had risen to approximately 60 per cent compared with 71 per cent for men. Also, in 1953, electoral abstentions were approximately 25 per cent among women and 13 per cent among men; by the 1978 legislative elections, 18.9 per cent of women voters abstained compared with 16.7 per cent of male voters. More recently, in the second round of the 1981 presidential elections, five per cent of women and six per cent of men voters abstained. Further evidence of increased politicisation can be seen in the greater willingness of women to state their party identification and preference. In 1958, 54.5 per cent of women had no response when asked to state their party preference, while in 1978 only 21.2 per cent failed to identify their party preference (40.5 and 17.6 per cent of male voters had no response in 1958 and 1978, respectively).[5]

While conservatism characterised the political preferences of French women through the first decade of the Fifth Republic, many began to show evidence of leftist partisanship from 1968 onward. In 1958, for example, only 24.7 per cent of women identified with a leftist party, and in the 1965 presidential elections General de Gaulle received an impressive 62 per cent of the female vote.[6] Yet, by 1978, 56 per cent of French women overall identified with a leftist party, a figure which was substantially higher among women under 30 years of age.[7] Taken together, increased politicisation and an electoral shift to the left among women helped to rejuvenate the French left generally during the 1970s and, later, to ensure a Socialist victory at the polls in 1981.

In contrast to their earlier reluctance, major leftist parties increasingly emphasised the mobilisation of women during the 1970s. The *Parti communiste français* (PCF) era of popular front politics followed by its Eurocommunist period were both characterised by efforts to mobilise women, which seemed to pay off as female PCF membership jumped from 25.5 per cent in 1966 to 32 per cent in 1976. Similarly, from its very beginnings in the aftermath of 1968, the PS attempted to mobilise women and established quotas within its party organisation (10 per cent in 1973, 25 per cent in 1979).[8] Notably, the PS share of the female vote jumped from 23.8 per cent in 1970 to 37.7 per cent in 1978, at the same time as female preferences for the PCF increased slightly.[9] The PS, in short, clearly benefited from increased politicisation and leftism among French women.

PS SUPPORT IN 1981

To a large extent, the new politics of the female electorate in 1981 were a product of the relative deprivation facing women in the labour force. Several important aspects of this situation – low status, high unemployment and inflation – encouraged women to support the Socialists in the hope that a new government would ameliorate the depressed economic conditions of working women. Although the latter increased from 34.7 per cent of the labour force in 1954 to 40 per cent in 1981, their ghettoisation in low-status, low-paid and low-mobility positions continued.[10] In 1974, for example, only 24 per cent of women were receiving employment training, a figure which rose only slightly to 28 per cent by 1981.[11] While women could choose among 30 fields of job specialisation, men could select from some 300, meaning that women remained confined to clerical or similarly designated 'female' sectors. As well, they remained clustered in part-time positions; in 1981, approximately 84 per cent of all part-time workers in France were women.[12] During the same period, approximately 75 per cent of minimum wage employees were women.[13] This lack of career opportunity and advancement in a society where women worked and sought work in unprecedented numbers provided them with a powerful incentive to consider economic change through political channels. As Mossuz-Lavau and Sineau (1983) suggest in their discussion of paid employment as an impetus toward political radicalisation,

> The political choices of women reflect well the place and the role they occupy in society. Adherence to the public sphere or the private sphere goes hand in hand with the expression of modernist or conservative values.[14]

One additional dimension of women's economic status was reflected in unemployment statistics. In 1981, the unemployment rate in France was 7.4 per cent (a total of about 2 million), but 60 per cent of those unemployed were women.[15] As in most Western nations, the problem of unemployment was especially acute for younger women;[16] approximately 70 per cent of women who sought work before the 1981 elections were 25 years of age or younger.[17] In the 18–25 year age group, 21 per cent of 'working' women were unemployed compared with 11 per cent of men.[18] And, not only was it more difficult for women to find work, but also they were laid off at a faster pace than men: between 1976 and 1981, the lay-off rate for women was 12 per cent per year, compared with 9 per cent for men.[19] This pattern, combined with job ghettoisation and unemployment, led many women to blame the Giscard government for economic ills which plagued France generally and women in particular.

The impact of inflation on French women compounded these factors. In 1977, the inflation rate was 10 per cent, but by 1981 it reached 13 per cent. Since women are responsible for roughly 83 per cent of consumer spending in France, the reality of frequent and major price increases was obvious as they shopped for food and other household necessities.[20]

Giscard's general social reforms were also subject to close scrutiny by an increasingly politicised female electorate. Many believed that the government's efforts – including the appointment of women to senior government posts – were either token, weakly applied or less than progressive. For example, Giscard established the following positions and charged them with the task of preparing 'a political response to the "preoccupations" of French women':[21]

1974: Secrétariat d'Etat à la Condition féminine
1976: Délégation nationale à la Condition féminine
1978: Secrétariat d'Etat chargé de l'emploi féminin
1980: Ministre délégué à la Condition féminine

Despite the creation of these various offices, however, the impact of women's concerns upon governmental activity was limited by the absence of clear policy mandates and implementation procedures.

In addition, the Giscard government endorsed reforms which would improve employment practices. These included 1975 legislation which called for non-discrimination in education, training and hiring, and for equal pay as a principle of law. The income differential between men and women remained 31 per cent, however, throughout 1981.

Reform of French abortion laws also occurred under the Giscard government, although left-wing opposition support for the 1979 legislation was essential since only 99 of the 291 majority deputies voted in favour.[22] Two specific provisions of the 1979 abortion law were widely criticised by women: first, the time limit on performing abortions and second, the cost. Under this reform legislation, pregnancies could be terminated only until the tenth week following conception, and the cost of abortions would not be paid by the state – two provisions which made French abortion law one of the most conservative in Western Europe. As the number of abortions in France rose from 170,000 in 1980 to 180,000 in 1981, concerns regarding legal termination and cost affected more and more women, such that the more liberal platform of the *Parti socialiste* in this area grew increasingly attractive to female electors.[23]

On 11 July 1975, the Giscard government passed new divorce legislation which recognised three grounds for divorce: mutual consent, a breakdown of marriage and divorce with fault. Though less restrictive than the previous law, this bill drew criticism from feminists who maintained that it needed to go further in easing the divorce process.[24]

The decline of traditional religiosity, which became very apparent by the 1970s, provided yet another reason for women to support the left in the 1981 elections. In 1956, 47 per cent of women were actively or regularly practising Catholics, compared with only 21 per cent in 1977; conversely, the proportion of inactively practising Catholics among women rose from 42 per cent in 1956 to 62 per cent in 1977.[25] Moreover, between 1974 and 1977 an estimated two million men and women left the Church. This secularisation of French society was accompanied by a 22 per cent decline in the number of priests between 1965 and 1975.[26] This decline in the influence of the Church may be attributed to rapid industrialisation and urbanisation; the coming of age of younger, better-educated cohorts; and the breakdown of a traditionally powerful communication network linking the Church with French society generally. As a group, these factors seemed to challenge the conventional – and largely conservative – political behaviour of French women.

A last, but nevertheless crucial, source of electoral change among French women rests in the organised feminist support base of the PS. By 1981, there were approximately 150 different feminist groups in France,[27] among the best-known of which was *psychanalyse et politique*, led by Antoinette Fouque and officially registered under the generic title and acronym of the *Mouvement de libération des femmes* (MLF). Using a considerable inheritance left to one of its supporters, *Psych et po* (or the 'official' women's movement, MLF-*déposé*) enhanced its public visibility through a weekly magazine, *Des femmes en mouvements hebdo* (with a circulation of some 150,000); a feminist bookstore in the heart of the Parisian Latin Quarter; and a feminist press known as *Des Femmes*. In the 1981 campaign, *Psych et po* publicly supported the *Parti socialiste*, and circulated posters which read: 'Women, the rising left is our place of identification and liberation. With François Mitterrand as President. Long live the MLF'.[28] Along with other feminist groups which opposed Giscard for reasons already discussed, *Psych et po* was able to sensitise and to inform both men and women concerning the problems facing women in a male-dominated world. As reflected in such books as Yvette Roudy's *La Femme en marge* (1975), feminists encouraged their readers and supporters to become more politically active, more critical of the policies of the Giscard government, and more willing to consider the PS as a promising alternative for the women of France.

THE PS OPTION

Mitterrand and the PS thus offered women, and particularly feminists, an opportunity to change the substantive directions of French government. Within the party élite, women comprised a legislated 10 per cent quota (Suresnes Congress 1973) later raised to 25 per cent (Metz Congress 1979). These quotas were designed to increase women's participation in the PS, such that by 1981 approximately 22 per cent of the Socialist membership of roughly 200,000 was female. In levels of party activity above the point of membership, the PS had more women in élite national offices and committees (19 per cent) than right-wing parties such as the Gaullist *Rassemblement pour la République* (RPR).[29] The PS also fielded more female candidates in national, regional, and local elections than either the RPR or the *Union démocratique français*(UDF), a practice which helped to convey the impression that the PS was quite serious about women's political participation as well as feminist issues.[30]

On the eve of the 1981 elections, the PS compiled a list of 110 policy positions, which became the party's campaign platform. At least 17 of these items dealt directly with the concerns of women; they included a 30 per cent minimum quota for women candidates in national, regional, and municipal elections; equal rights in employment and equal pay provisions;

improved access to contraception and legal abortion; and expanded day-care facilities.[31]

Also before the election, the PS published a book entitled *Projet socialiste pour la France des années 80*. This work reflected in part the impact of discussions among feminists within the PS, who presented a *Manifeste sur les droits des femmes* at the 1979 Metz party congress. Although some have claimed that the *Projet socialiste* reflects a less than serious discussion of women's needs (only 17 of its 380 pages deal specifically with women), the work was intended to integrate the question of women's future within a broader framework of the economic crisis in France and the socialist response to it.[32] The *Projet* thus discusses improving the status of women in reference to men and women as equal beneficiaries of the socialist plan: 'First Priority, Social Growth, the Right to Work; Second Priority, Responsible Men and Women; Third Priority, The Time and the Interest to Live; Fourth Priority, An Independent France Open to the World'.[33]

On a more individual level, Mitterrand projected a progressive image as the PS presidential candidate. On the eve of the first round of the 1981 elections, the prominent feminist group *Choisir* invited all four major presidential candidates – Mitterrand, Marchais, Giscard and Chirac – to discuss their views on the status of women. The only candidate to accept this invitation was Mitterrand, who used the occasion to discuss a broad range of women's issues with feminist leaders. Excerpts from this 'debate' were later broadcast on French radio and television. Overall, Mitterrand appeared to be well-informed and sensitive to women's condition, stating his intention to include more female ministers in his government, to improve the professional training of women, to reduce the pay differentials between men and women, to establish more day care centres and to provide public funding of abortions. *Choisir* published this discussion in book form before the elections under the title *Which President for Women? The Responses of François Mitterrand*, which made it clear that the organisation endorsed Mitterrand and encouraged women in general to support him.[34]

By way of contrast, major economic problems in France, as well as the Bokassa diamond scandal and the government's handling of a terrorist attack on the Jewish synagogue on the Rue Copernic, plagued the Giscard campaign. Coupled with growing female politicisation and leftism, these factors helped to make the 1981 French presidential elections a watershed not only for women, but also for the political system as a whole. Overall, some 52 per cent of female voters supported Mitterrand[35] – the first time in French history that a majority of women voted for the left.[36] Later, in the legislative elections of June 1981, a similar percentage of women voted for the leftist bloc and the PS won an absolute majority of seats in the National Assembly, marking the first time since the French Revolution that both executive and legislative power was controlled by the left. Furthermore, the 1981 Assembly included 5.9 per cent women members, a level which is low by wider European standards but which constitutes the greatest ever female representation in the Assembly. Prime Minister Pierre Mauroy observed subsequently, 'For the first time in May and June [of 1981], a majority of women voted for a leftist President of the Republic and Assembly'.[37] Women had thus largely made possible the 1981 Socialist election victory.

THE PS IN POWER

The leftist government led by Mitterrand sponsored a host of neo-Keynesian reforms during its first year in office, including a 10 per cent increase in the minimum wage; a reduction in hours worked per week; an increase in family, elderly and handicapped allowances; and an extension of paid vacations from four to five weeks per year. Women also benefited from the creation of more than 100,000 new jobs in the public sector and from increased child-care facilities (though not to the extent promised before the elections).[38] A separate Ministry of Women's Rights was established under the leadership of Yvette Roudy, a socialist feminist whose share of the national budget was far greater than that of her predecessor. Notably, Roudy's ministry received 109 million *francs* in 1984, an 8.2 per cent increase over 1983, at a time when the national budget increase was only 6.2 per cent.[39] Roudy was given veto authority over all government legislation affecting women, power which she viewed as reflective of the PS commitment to change:

> For the first time in Europe, the rights of women have become in France – with the existence of a ministry provided with a budget – a government component, a political design clearly included in a global project of change. The fight against sexism and the inequalities which follow is no longer the isolated fact of a handful of women. This fight is taken into the broader field of reduction of all inequalities.[40]

In addition to Roudy's position as Minister of Women's Rights, Mitterrand appointed five other women to his 44-member cabinet: Nicole Questiaux (PS) as Minister of National Solidarity, Edith Cresson (PS) as Minister of Agriculture, Edwige Avice (PS) as Delegate Minister under the Minister of Recreation charged with youth and sports, Catherine Lalumière (PS) as Minister of Consumer Affairs, and Georgina Dufoix (PS) as Secretary of State for National Solidarity responsible for the family. The appointment of these six women meant that women represented 14 per cent of the Mitterrand cabinet, a level far exceeding that of previous governments. In particular, the appointment of a woman as Minister of Agriculture was considered important because this position had long been considered a 'man's job'. At the same time, Mitterrand hired a personal staff which included 216 women, compared with 176 under Giscard.[41] The President emphasised the importance of these various measures in an International Women's Day speech in which he stated:

> There remains not only to reinforce the rights of women but especially to make them reality. Such is the task that I confer upon the Minister of Women's Rights. But this task involves equally all other members of the government.[42]

In late 1982, the government attempted to fulfil its promise concerning state funding for abortion. After a year and a half of vacillation and delay, the Assembly voted on 20 December to reimburse 80 per cent of abortion costs through the social security system. While all but two of the 286 PS deputies and all 44 PCF deputies voted in favour of reimbursement, only one member of the opposition, a UDF deputy, supported it.[43] Although some feminists maintained that the reimbursement should be 100 per cent as it is in many other European countries, the PS/PCF action in December 1982 represented a major victory for the women's movement over the opponents of government funding.

Overall, the record of the Socialist government on women's issues cannot be separated from its broader policy context, involving a number of financial miscalculations and general emphasis upon economic restraint. During 1981–82, a 'reflation in one country' policy was pursued which allocated large sums for a number of reforms, many of which directly and indirectly aided women. This reflationary policy, however, failed to work as the inflation rate rose and the national debt increased. By June of 1982, the government was forced to do an about-face and to adopt an austerity programme, a *plan de rigueur*, that intensified in March 1983 following leftist losses in the municipal elections of that year. This abrupt switch to austerity was accompanied by a warning from Jacques Delors, the Minister of Finance: 'There can be no expensive reforms in 1983 or 1984'.[44] This policy clearly curtailed a number of reforms proposed by the Ministry of Women's Rights, to which we now turn our attention.

THE MINISTRY OF WOMEN'S RIGHTS

The creation of a Ministry of Women's Rights with a budget in excess of 100,000,000 francs helped to advance the rights of women both within government and among the French public generally. In a very short period of time, Yvette Roudy's work as an articulate and highly visible minister created a style of operation, known as the 'Roudy Effect', which was envied and emulated by other government departments.[45] According to one IFOP poll conducted in December 1983, 79 per cent of men and women had heard about the Ministry of Women's Rights, and 77 per cent of both sexes considered it to be necessary.[46] In fact, Roudy's energetic, articulate and dedicated support of women's rights led one source to describe her as the '100,000-volt lady'.[47]

Born on 10 April 1929 in Pessac near Bordeaux, Yvette Roudy was one of three children raised in a distinctively working-class milieu. Referring to this family background, Roudy once remarked that she knew the 'class struggle before the sex struggle'.[48] Her career began at the age of 16, when she worked as a stenographer/typist for a wine agent. Later, after marrying Pierre Roudy, she lived in Glasgow for two years and studied English to a standard which enabled her to translate *The Feminine Mystique* into French. When Betty Friedan's book appeared in France in 1965, it became an important source of inspiration for the nascent French feminist movement and for Roudy personally. She thus played a leading role in the 1964 Democratic Women's Movement, founded and served as editor-in-chief of

Women of the 20th Century, and participated in one club precursor of the PS (CIR). Following the establishment of the PS, Roudy developed its feminist action programme by helping to draft a manifesto of women's rights and by standing as a Socialist candidate in the 1978 legislative elections. During this same period Roudy published *La Femme en marge* (1975), with a preface by François Mitterrand; the book enhanced her reputation as a leading socialist feminist in France and Western Europe generally.[49] From 1979 to 1981, she served as a French representative to the European Parliament and eventually headed its Commission on the Rights of Women. This background made her a natural choice for the new French ministry which was created in 1981.

Several weeks after accepting her appointment, Roudy held a press conference where she announced that the main objectives of the Ministry were as follows: first, to enhance the salaries, employment opportunities and professional training of women; second, to improve access to contraception and abortion; third, to disseminate information about women's issues; and fourth, to oppose sexism generally in order to increase the power and autonomy of women. The central theme of Roudy's presentation was that she wanted to expand the use of 'positive discrimination', otherwise known as affirmative action, which the *Parti socialiste* had introduced earlier in its internal quotas for female participation.[50]

In response to her first objective, Roudy drafted landmark legislation on labour force equality. Before this law was passed in July 1983, Roudy organised a national campaign to sensitise men and women to gender-based inequality in the workplace and, in particular, to the importance of career planning and guidance for younger women. (Many younger women are trained to work in clerical, health science, and other areas severely affected by unemployment.)[51] The new law enacted in 1983, commonly referred to as the 'Roudy Law,' was an effort to strengthen the rights of women in the workplace. A press communiqué issued by the Minister of Women's Rights described the new legislation as follows:

> The Roudy Law is not content with establishing equality of rights. It proposes equally that there be established in business as well as in professional fields catch-up measures in the realm of access to employment, of training sufficient to offer women equal opportunities in their professional life.[52]

The basic provisions of the Roudy Law included an end to gender discrimination in employment, guarantees of equal treatment except during periods of pregnancy and childbirth, and permission for unions to bring women's grievances before a court. As well, the law makes it possible for judges to require that employers create a plan for gender equality within their enterprises, and establishes a watchdog organisation – the Supervisory Council for Professional Equality – to ensure that the law requiring equal access to training is implemented. More than any provision, this last element distinguishes the Professional Equality Law from earlier legislative efforts by the Giscard government and its Ministry for the Condition of Women.

The enforcement arm of the Roudy Law, the Supervisory Council for

Professional Equality, was officially created on 16 July 1984 in the presence of Prime Minister Pierre Mauroy. At this ceremony, Mauroy condemned society's double standard:

> The situation of women still does not conform to their wishes. Too many handicaps, too many obstacles persist ... There is, as a result, what I would be tempted to call a sort of double market: one for men, another second-class one for women. It constitutes a form of social injustice and a waste of resources and abilities. To strive toward the objective of equality is not only an act of social justice. It is also an act of *economic rationalisation*.[53]

Not only did the creation of the Supervisory Council constitute a vast improvement over earlier efforts to implement equality in employment, but also its basic assumption that the integration of women within the labour force is an economic necessity was radically different from older conservative and liberal beliefs that female employment was in part to blame for rising unemployment. In the face of a severe economic crisis as well as growing conservatism among French voters, Mauroy's statement seemed especially courageous. The passage of the Roudy Law thus suggested that the PS government was serious about making employers more accountable and sensitive to their female employees, expanding training programmes (women currently constitute only 29 per cent of those engaged in in-service training programmes),[54] creating more job opportunities, and reducing the income inequalities between working men and women. At the installation ceremony of the Supervisory Council, Roudy emphasised the significance of the Law on Professional Equality: 'Need I remind you ... how much this ... places us at the forefront of European countries in this domain?'[55]

In her ministerial role as well, Roudy has actively encouraged the European Economic Community to address the common unemployment problems facing women across Europe. By the summer of 1984, unemployment within the EEC member nations was considerably higher for women than men: 11.4 against 8.7 per cent.[56] Partly as a result of Roudy's pressure, the EEC Council of Ministers adopted a resolution in June 1984 to work towards reducing female unemployment.[57]

On the second goal of improved access to contraception and abortion, the Ministry of Women's Rights sponsored a nation-wide campaign to encourage family planning, a project which Mitterrand had supported despite controversies since 1965.[58] Roudy's campaign during 1981 and following used strategically-placed posters in subways and trains as well as prime-time television advertisements to publicise telephone numbers which could provide additional information. In addition, approximately 1,000,000 copies of a brochure on contraceptive usage were distributed; this effort was especially significant because the French public had previously been denied easy access to contraceptive information and, in fact, the advertisement of contraceptives had long remained illegal. After only one year of the campaign, family planning consultations doubled[59] and 88 new family planning centres were created.[60] The success of this campaign can be illuminated further by considering that when Roudy assumed office in 1981, only 37 per cent of French women practised any modern form of contraception.[61]

Roudy also attempted to ensure that the PS would fulfil its campaign promise to provide fully subsidised abortions. Given the wider French economic crisis and inter-ministerial politics, a December 1982 statute granted only 80 per cent reimbursement for abortions – a compromise which was unsatisfactory for both French feminists and for the credibility of the PS regime. As noted above, many feminists had hoped for swift action to provide 100 per cent reimbursement for abortion costs. The law was later strengthened by a provision which increased the number of hospitals formally certified to perform this procedure.[62]

The dissemination of information about women's issues was yet another goal announced by Roudy in 1981. In this area, her ministry has proved creative and active, aided by the fact that approximately 30 per cent of its budget is directed specifically toward the dissemination of information. One of the first activities undertaken by Roudy in 1981 was the creation of a commission, headed by historian Madeleine Robérieux, to study the status of women in France. The report of this commission, published in book form in 1982, included a review of the inequalities facing women in France and offered a comprehensive guide to the problem areas which Roudy and her ministry would need to address. The report thus provided both the public and the government with a detailed account of the condition of women in contemporary France.

One of the major ways in which Roudy's ministry attempted to disseminate information and to raise public consciousness on key issues was through the use of national media campaigns. In this respect, efforts to increase knowledge and use of contraceptives and to implement equality in employment were highly visible and effective publicity vehicles, as was yet another national campaign launched in April 1984 to enhance the professional orientation of younger women. This last effort was designed to encourage younger women to consider non-traditional occupations when planning their careers.

Parallel with its various media campaigns, the ministry established approximately 140 National Centres for Information on the Rights of Women (CNIDF) throughout France. These centres not only help to link the ministry in Paris with the rest of the country, but also serve as resource centres for women who require advice and counselling in such areas as professional training, wife-battering, rape and prostitution.[63] The creation of CNIDFs has increased the ministry's visibility and support among the female population, at the same time as it has helped to establish a new type of ministerial structure which will not be easily dismantled should a change of government occur.

Related to both the media campaigns and CNIDFs are a series of Ministry publications produced since 1981. They include a monthly bulletin entitled *Citoyennes à part entière*, with a circulation of 30,000, which provides information on current issues affecting women in France. The ministry has also released a series of bulletins concerning the condition of French women: *Guide to the Rights of Women; Contraception – A Fundamental Right; Talk*

About It, But Where?: Love, Contraception, and Sexuality; Guide to the Rights of Single Women; Professional Equality Between Women and Men; Guide to Work Rights; Where to Have Your Baby in Paris; and *Guide to Women's Associations.* Additional bulletins have been planned on such topics as employment and training, immigrant women and the abandoned wives of foreigners. These publications as well as posters and other brochures are disseminated through the national network of Information Centres, at the Ministry offices in Paris, and through a special mailing address.

Closely linked to its publication programme are the research projects undertaken by the Ministry of Women's Rights, which have examined the impact of high technology and government policy on female employment, prostitution, women prisoners, immigrant women, sexual mutilation among African immigrants, and women and culture.[64] To facilitate further feminist research, the ministry subsidises the Centre for Feminist Research and Information as well as the Simone de Beauvoir Audio-Visual Centre. Roudy's ministry and the Ministry of Research have also established a joint three-year grant programme for women researchers which, it is hoped, will generate additional knowledge and policy options in the field of women's issues.

A more general opposition to sexism is reflected in a variety of reforms proposed by the ministry. As well as the Law on Professional Equality, Roudy sponsored anti-sexism legislation which was approved by the Council of Ministers in March 1983. This law, supported by Mitterrand, was based on the principle that sexism, like racism, is undesirable, offensive, and provokes discrimination, hatred and violence. Since the French government had adopted an anti-racism law in 1972, both Roudy and Mitterrand believed that by 1983 the time had come for a similar law against sexism.[65] A number of women's groups shared this view and organised to support such a law; they included the League of Women's Rights, SOS Women's Alternatives, Family Planning, the Simone de Beauvoir Audio-Visual Centre and the Carabosse Bookstore.[66]

What specifically were these groups supporting? The proposed law challenged sexism on the job and in the media; it allowed women to appeal against discriminatory hiring practices through the legal process and to sue magazines, newspapers and advertisers who presented degrading portrayals of women. This latter provision caused a furore in the French press and among advertisers.

Since the controversial nature of the sexism law thus generated considerable (free) publicity, Roudy spent little of her own budget on advertising. *Le Monde, Libération*, and other major newspapers devoted front-page coverage to the issue, although their treatment was generally hostile, referring to Roudy as 'Yvette, or the Ridiculous Puritan', 'Roudy the Moralist', and 'the Decrees of Madame Ayatollah'.[67] While many journalists thus saw the bill as a threat to freedom of expression, advertisers argued that it would harm their economic well-being. The Ministry of Women's Rights nevertheless stood its ground and calmly defended the anti-sexism legislation. According to a 1983 issue of *Citoyennes*,

It is not a project of censure that would pose an attack on the legitimate freedom of the press. The freedom of the press is fully respected. But it is normal that in the case of abuse, the law defends another freedom just as fundamental – that which permits citizens to legally act to uphold the dignity of the individual ... It acts then as a law of freedom because the freedom of some stops where that of others begins.[68]

In fact, a SOFRES poll conducted in April 1983 suggested that the anti-sexism law was generally viewed favourably among those respondents who held an opinion: 42 per cent favoured the law, 16 per cent were opposed to it, and 39 per cent indifferent.[69] Nevertheless, the persistence and power of sexism in French politics and society was revealed when the bill was lost in the National Assembly – apparently because many of its members did not share the commitments of Roudy and Mitterrand.

Two other projects have thus been initiated to fight sexism somewhat differently. First, the Ministry has begun an effort to eliminate references and images which sexualise and stereotype women in school textbooks. A special commission has been created through the co-operative efforts of the Ministry of Women's Rights and the Ministry of Education to examine textbooks and to determine the extent to which they must be revised in order to obtain an equal and positive representation of both women and men. The Ministry of Education has also been encouraged to sensitise trainee teachers regarding the images of men and women which they present in the classroom, and has introduced a number of audio-visual programmes for this purpose.

Second, the Women's Rights Ministry has attempted to reform the sexist bias of the French language more generally. For example, the expression for 'human rights' is *'droits de l'homme'* – the rights of man. Pointing to the fact that francophone Quebec uses the more neutral *'droits de la personne'* (rights of the person), feminists argue that such neutral expressions need to be introduced in France wherever possible, particularly in the field of education. According to Roudy, 'The school is precisely ... the place of socialisation of children – it inculcates them ...',[70] and often in subtle linguistic fashion.

She has thus established a Commission on Terminology for the Feminisation of Names and Titles, headed by author Benoîte Groult and charged with a mandate to achieve equal rights in French language usage. There is limited consensus among feminists concerning the best means towards this end; for her part, Roudy has proposed that feminine equivalents be applied to the names and titles of all professions held by men and women. Her own job, for example, carries a masculine title – Madame *le* Ministre – which, Roudy contends, implies that such a position is properly held only by a man. Even a simple change of article in Roudy's title, indeed, opposed by many who argue that the masculine article is sufficiently neutral, would add a peculiar irony to the position because the phrase Madame *la* Ministre refers not to a female minister but to the wife of the minister.

Aware of the difficult mandate facing her language reform commission, Benoîte Groult has commented:

WOMEN, POLITICS AND THE FRENCH SOCIALISTS 63

> It is in the spirit of equality and of justice that the work of the Commission must be undertaken; its results, we know, risk throwing into confusion a usage which in 1984 is profoundly anachronistic.[71]

Roudy has also noted this controversy, reminding her supporters and opponents alike that the French language has at times been consciously altered to reflect changing social realities:

> The revolutionaries of 1789 decided to replace 'monsieur' and 'madame' with 'citizen' because they knew very well that language does not only vaguely reflect political ideas, but that it can create and modify ... our behaviour.[72]

The problem, of course, is that the contemporary 'revolution' in question is led primarily by women, who challenge male authorities that remain averse to, and indeed unwilling to accept, change in language. Some feminists thus maintain that objections to language reform are essentially misogyny camouflaged by tradition and custom.[73] Whether because of sincere interest in the purity of the French language or misogynist contempt, then, strong opposition to the recommendations of the Groult Commission is likely.

Finally, the Ministry of Women's Rights has worked to weaken sexism and to enhance the power and autonomy of women through a series of legislative initiatives. In June 1982, a law was enacted permitting women with children whose fathers had not made support payments to receive government stipends; moreover, alimony laws were strengthened to aid divorced women generally. In 1983, a finance law was passed eliminating the concept of 'head of household', and requiring both spouses to sign all family tax forms.[74] This recognition of women as equal partners, rather than dependants, in family financial matters was crucial in providing increased power and autonomy.

These comprehensive efforts in four main policy areas reflect Roudy's energetic commitment to the improvement of women's rights in France. Their impact must be measured, however, with reference to the more general political fate of French women under the PS government.

WOMEN AND POLITICS SINCE 1981

The establishment of an assertive and innovative Ministry of Women's Rights under the leadership of Yvette Roudy has itself been a significant accomplishment of the PS government. By providing new public services such as national information centres, improved state funding for abortions, and family planning facilities, the commitment of the PS government to women has been revealed.

Women have also made more identifiably political gains since the 1981 elections. For example, the internal PS quota for women has brought their numbers to approximately 21 per cent of the total party membership;[75] in addition, six women sat in the 1981 Mitterrand government cabinet, and the proportion of female members in the National Assembly in 1984 was greater than at any point since French women received the right to vote in 1944. Although the most dramatic increase in female parliamentary representation occurred in 1978, the number of women in the Assembly has neither stabilised nor decreased, but is growing steadily. The 1986 Assembly elections, which should be held under the terms of a new 30 per cent quota rule, will shed important light on this trend.

On the regional and local levels, party quotas for female candidates have helped women to make additional political gains. In 1979, Giscard d'Estaing proposed that parties permit no more than 80 per cent of their municipal candidates to be of the same gender. Although Prime Minister Raymond Barre did not register this project as law, most parties of the left adhered to its terms and included a large proportion of women candidates in the 1979 EEC parliamentary lists: 27.2 per cent in the PCF and 25.9 per cent in the PS, compared with 20.9 per cent in the UDF and 16 per cent in the Gaullist RPR. Female representation in the French delegation to the European Parliament thus increased to 22 per cent compared with four per cent in the National Assembly and only three per cent in the Senate.[76]

TABLE 1
WOMEN MUNICIPAL COUNCILLORS AND MAYORS IN FRANCE, 1947–1983

Year	Women Municipal Councillors No.	%	Women Mayors No.	%
1947	14,889	3.1	250	0.7
1953	13,832	2.7	300	0.8
1959	11,246	2.4	381	1.0
1965	11,145	2.3	421	1.1
1971	20,684	4.4	696	1.8
1977	38,304	8.3	1,018	2.8
1983	70,155	14.0	1,445	4.0

Source: *Citoyennes*, May 1983, p.9.

The Mitterrand government also endorsed a 30 per cent quota for women candidates in the municipal elections of March 1983. As a result of this quota rule and the enhanced politicisation of French women generally, female candidates in 1983 made a major breakthrough on the municipal level, especially in the number of local councillors elected to office (see Table 1).[77]

At the same time as women have entered the political life of France, though, their economic participation has been limited by a seriously ailing economy. Roudy's efforts to strengthen professional opportunities available to younger women hold promise for the longer term, yet, at present, women bear a disproportionate burden for France's ongoing economic crisis. For example, 55 per cent of those unemployed in 1984 were female, and 25 per cent of women under the age of 25 were out of work. Although the former figure represents some improvement over the 60 per cent of unemployed who were female in 1981, the actual number of unemployed has grown steadily such that roughly the same number of women were out of work in 1984 as in 1981.[78]

Popular support for the Mitterrand government, including among women, has weakened as a result of these problems. The implementation of an austerity programme (*plan de rigueur*), combined with efforts to modernise French heavy industry produced schisms within the governing PS and ultimately led to a PCF withdrawal from the *union de la gauche* in July 1984. In claiming to be the uncompromising defender of workers' rights, the PCF explained its decision as follows: 'We do not have the moral right to allow millions of disappointed and worried women, men, and youths to believe that we could, in this government, respond to their needs'.[79] In suggesting that the Socialists had ignored the needs of the French people, the PCF further deepened popular impressions that the PS government had lost touch with the realities both of the economy and of public opinion. Survey results indicated the extent of this growing distrust: shortly after taking office in 1981, President Mitterrand enjoyed the confidence of 74 per cent of the French public and Prime Minister Mauroy of 71 per cent. By June 1984, however, Mitterrand's confidence rating had fallen to about 30 per cent, the lowest of any president in the Fifth Republic, while Mauroy's had also reached an all-time low of 25 per cent. Moreover, poll results indicated that Mitterrand's confidence rating declined more quickly among women than men.[80]

Not only did French voters lose confidence in the ability of leaders of the left to govern the country, but they also reflected growing pessimism about the future. In November 1982, 37 per cent of women and 42 per cent of men polled expressed confidence in the left. By June 1983, however, women's confidence level had dropped to 22 per cent compared with 30 per cent for men. During this same period, women and men demonstrated growing confidence in the right, a phenomenon which may be linked with increasing pessimism about the future among many voters.[81] According to one SOFRES poll conducted in November 1982, 53 per cent of women and 49 per cent of men were pessimistic about the future; one year later, 66 per cent of women and 57 per cent of men expressed pessimism.[82] Since the second SOFRES survey corresponds with the announcement by the PS government of its *plan de rigueur*, there would seem to be a strong correlation between the introduction of an austerity programme, on the one hand, and popular loss of confidence in the PS leadership and the future more generally, on the other. Indeed, many male and female voters displayed their discontent in a concrete way by voting for opposition parties in European parliamentary elections.

As reported in Table 2, French voters in 1984 heavily favoured the EEC opposition list headed by Simone Veil. Notably, eight per cent more women than men voted for Veil in this election, while men more heavily favoured the extreme right headed by Le Pen (13 per cent against eight per cent). If the EEC election can be considered to reflect broader partisan beliefs in

TABLE 2
FRENCH PARTY VOTE BY GENDER (%),
1984 EUROPEAN PARLIAMENTARY ELECTIONS

Party List	PCF	PS	Opposition	Extreme Right	
Leader	Marchais	Jospin	Veil	Le Pen	Other
Men	12	22	39	13	14
Women	10	20	47	8	15
Total	11	21	43	11	14

Source: Le Nouvel Observateur, 22–28 June 1984, p. 24.

TABLE 3
FRENCH VOTE BY EMPLOYMENT STATUS (%), 1984 EEC ELECTIONS

	Employed		Housewife	Unemployed		Retired		Student	
	M	W	W	M	W	M	W	M	W
PCF	12	11	8	13	16	15	11	5	4
PS	21	21	16	21	23	21	21	16	24
Opposition	38	42	52	25	31	46	54	31	42
Nat. Front	14	9	10	21	10	12	8	13	5
Other	15	17	14	20	20	6	6	35	25

Source: IFOP poll in Le Monde, 15 August 1984.

France (notably, the abstention rate exceeded 40 per cent), then both women and men would seem to have moved distinctly towards the right.
Additional 1984 data, reported in Table 3, show that the PS was supported to roughly the same extent (21–24 per cent) by employed, retired, unemployed and student women, while its base was weaker among housewives (16 per cent). Women as a group remained less favourable towards the PCF than men (except among the unemployed, where 16 per cent of women and 13 per cent of men voted PCF) – a pattern which also occurred in support for Le Pen's extreme right wing list. The overall 1984 results represented the first time since 1969 that the combined parties of the left had received less than 40 per cent of the vote, and the first time since 1973 that the PS received less than 21 per cent. For the PCF, these results were especially humiliating given that the party had not fallen to the 11 per cent since 1928.[83]
In addition to their ability to capitalise on the economic crisis confronting the Mitterrand government, the opposition parties used the volatile *école libre* issue (public funding of mainly private religious schools) to consolidate

popular opposition to the government. In attempting to gain greater state control over *école libre* staff personnel, the Socialist government incurred the anger of about a million demonstrators who rallied in Paris against a proposed education reform bill in July 1984, just one week after the EEC elections.[84] Shortly thereafter, Mitterrand's government temporarily withdrew this legislation, re-organised its cabinet assignments and attempted to regain public confidence and support.

CONCLUSION

This study has examined some of the major reasons for and political consequences of women's increased politicisation and leftist partisanship in post-war France. Increased integration into French society has transformed the female electorate into a powerful voting bloc which not only passes judgement on the PS and its handling of the French economic crisis, but also may decide the fate of the left in the future. At the time of writing, women would seem to be returning as a group to centre and centre/right parties and candidates – a trend which suggests that their partisanship is not inexorably fixed to either the left or to the right. Rather, contemporary French voters, regardless of gender, seem to be primarily influenced by economic conditions. Therefore, as the integration of women into the economic life of France increases, we may expect voting patterns among men and women to continue to converge.[85]

In addition, the virtual institutionalisation of the women's movement in France could also be expected to narrow gender differences in political behaviour. Women are no longer strictly confined to the margins of the political process; yet, as the experiences of Roudy and the Ministry of Women's Rights indicate, women may now be a captive of their very success within the PS. That is, the grass-roots women's movement has weakened, having been replaced in large part by the new ministry which is itself dependent upon the broader future (both economic and political) of the Mitterrand government.

Despite the financial restraints on the Ministry of Women's Rights, Roudy has enjoyed considerable personal and issue support: 89 per cent of the public endorsed the professional equality law, 76 per cent the creation of the CNIDFs, 62 per cent the partial state funding of abortion, and 86 per cent the national campaign for contraception,[86] at a time when Mitterrand and the PS generally have experienced a serious crisis of public confidence. The popularity of Roudy and her ministry, contrasted with the precipitous fall in the level of public confidence in the Socialist government, provides further evidence that women's contemporary priorities as voters are primarily economic and only secondarily concerned with 'women's issues'.

Since women now comprise more than 40 per cent of the workforce and 53 per cent of the voting population in France, political parties and personalities can no longer underestimate their political awareness and power. If Mitterrand and the *Parti Socialiste* hope to prevent major electoral setbacks in the 1986 legislative and 1988 presidential elections, then they will require the decisive support of women voters. The future of socialism in France may rest, therefore, in the ability of the Mitterrand government to ameliorate the deep-seated economic crisis and to address women as full citizens.

NOTES

1. The authors thank several staff members of the *Ministère des Droits de la femme* for their research assistance. Yvonne Lochey, press secretary to Yvette Roudy, provided us with a significant amount of published and unpublished information concerning the work of the ministry. A lengthy conversation with Catherine Beauvois, the liaison between the ministry and the European Parliament, gave us insights into the past, present, and future projects of the *Ministère des Droits de la femme*.
2. See Wayne Northcutt, 'The Election of François Mitterrand and the *Parti socialiste* in France: The Making of a *Phénomène socialiste*', *Australian Journal of Politics and History* 28:2 (1982), pp. 218–35; and Wayne Northcutt and Jeffra Flaitz, 'Women and Politics in Contemporary France: The Electoral Shift to the Left in the 1981 Presidential and Legislative Elections, *Contemporary French Civilization* 7:2 (Winter 1983), pp. 183–98.
3. Sylvia B. Bashevkin, 'Changing Patterns of Politicization and Partisanship Among Women in France', *British Journal of Political Science* 15:1 (January 1985), pp. 77–9.
4. Ibid, pp. 79–83.
5. Ibid, pp. 93–5. See also *Le Nouvel Observateur*, 1–7 June 1981 and 4–10 July 1981.
6. Northcutt and Flaitz, 'Women and Politics in Contemporary France', p. 183.
7. Bashevkin, 'Changing Patterns', Table 7.
8. Janine Mossuz-Lavau and Mariette Sineau, *Enquête sur les femmes et la politique* (Paris: Presses Universitaires de France, 1983), p. 11.
9. Bashevkin, 'Changing Patterns', p. 95. For a discussion of women and the union movement in France in the 1970s, see Jane Jenson, 'The "Problem" of Women', in Mark Kesselman (ed.), *The French Workers' Movement* (London: Allen & Unwin, 1984), pp. 159–76.
10. *Des Femmes en mouvements*, 5–12 June 1981, p. 6. See also Janine Mossuz-Lavau and Mariette Sineau, *Les Femmes françaises en 1978: Insertion sociale, insertion politique* (Paris: CNRS, 1980).
11. Gisèle Halimi, *Quel Président pour les femmes? Réponses de François Mitterrand* (Paris: Gallimard, 1981), p. 44.
12. Ibid, p. 59.
13. Yvette Roudy, *La Femme en marge* (Paris: Flammarion, 1982), p. 23.
14. Mossuz-Lavau and Sineau, *Enquête*, p. 79.
15. For a discussion of economic problems in France on the eve of the 1981 elections, see Wayne Northcutt, *The French Socialist and Communist Party Under the Fifth Republic, 1958–1981: From Opposition to Power* (New York: Irvington Publishers, 1985); and Guillemette de Sairigué, *Les Françaises face au chômage* (Paris: Denoël/Gonthier, 1978).
16. Halimi, *Quel Président*, p. 42.
17. Gisèle Halimi, *Le Programme Commun des femmes* (Paris: Grasset, 1978), p. 105. See also *Le Monde*, 4 August 1982.
18. Mossuz-Lavau and Sineau, *Enquête*, p. 265.
19. *Des Femmes en mouvements*, 5–12 June 1981, p. 6.
20. Halimi, *Le Programme Commun*, p. 105.
21. *Les Femmes en France dans une société d'inégalités: Rapport au ministre des Droits de la femme* (Paris: La Documentation Française, 1982), p. 175.
22. Gordon Shenton, 'The Advancement of Women in Giscard d'Estaing's Advanced Liberal Society', *The Massachusetts Review*, 17:4 (Winter, 1976), p. 760.
23. *Le Monde*, 3 August 1982.
24. *L'Express*, 13–19 December 1980, p. 139.
25. Notably, housewives were twice as numerous among practising Catholics as non-housewives. See Mossuz-Lavau and Sineau, *Enquête*, p. 62.
26. Ibid, p. 243. See also *Le Nouvel Observateur*, 23–29 January 1978, pp. 51–70, and 30 January–5 February 1978, pp. 53–5; and R. W. Johnson, *The Long March of the French Left* (New York: St. Martin's, 1981), pp. 112–13.
27. See *Le Nouvel Observateur*, 25–31 July 1981.

28. See Dorothy Kaufmann-McCall, 'Politics of Difference: The Women's Movement in France from May 1968 to Mitterrand', *Signs* 9:2 (Winter 1983), pp. 282–93.
29. *Rapport au ministre des Droits de la femme*, p. 174.
30. Ibid.
31. See Pierre Mauroy, *C'est ici le chemin* (Paris: Flammarion, 1982), pp. 219–47 and Dennis MacShane, *François Mitterrand: A Political Odyssey* (London: Quartet Books, 1982), pp. 259–73.
32. See Yvonne Rochette Ozzello and Elaine Marks, 'Mignonnes, allons voir sous la rose ... Socialism, Feminism and Misogyny in the France of Yvette Roudy: May 1981–May 1983', *Contemporary French Civilization* 8:1–2 (Fall/Winter 1983–84).
33. See Parti Socialiste, *Projet socialiste pour la France des années 80* (Paris: Club socialiste du livre, n.d.).
34. See Halimi, *Quel Président*.
35. *Des Femmes en mouvements*, 5–12 June 1981, pp. 18–19.
36. Ibid, p. 19. According to *Des Femmes en mouvements*, differences between male and female vote for the left decreased significantly between 1965 and 1981:

Year	Election	Gender difference (%)
1965	Presidential	12
1973	Legislative	9
1974	Municipal	7
1977	Municipal	4
1978	Legislative	6
1981	Presidential	0

37. Mauroy as quoted in *Citoyennes à part entière: bulletin d'information sur les droits des femmes* (October 1982), p. 14.
38. In explaining the government's inability to provide the number of new day-care centres promised before the 1981 elections, Mitterrand argued that they 'are expensive to build and to administer and available state funds have been reduced'. See *Hommes et Libertés: Journal de la Ligue des Droits de l'Homme*, no. 33 (1984), p. 6.
39. *Citoyennes*, May 1984, p. 4.
40. Roudy as quoted in ibid, p. 3.
41. Ozzello and Marks, 'Sous la rose', p. 210.
42. Mitterrand as quoted in *Citoyennes*, May 1984, p. 4.
43. Alain Lancelot and Marie-Thérèse Lancelot, *Annuaire de la France Politique* (Paris: Presses de la Fondation Nationale des Sciences Politiques, 1984), p. 44.
44. See Wayne Northcutt, 'The Changing Domestic Policies and Views of the Mitterrand Government, 1981–1984: The Crisis of Contemporary French Socialism', *Contemporary French Civilization* (Spring/Summer 1985).
45. Michelle Coquillat, *Qui sont-elles*, reported in Ministère des Droits de la femme, *Service de Presse: Bilan des actions* (1984).
46. *Citoyennes*, May 1984, pp. 4–5.
47. Geneviève Dermech, 'Madame cent mille volts', *La Voix du Nord* (29 May 1981), reported in Ministère des Droits de la femme, *Dossier: Bilan* (1984).
48. Coquillat, *Qui sont-elles*.
49. For biographical information on Roudy, see excerpt from *Nouveau dictionnaire biographique européen* reported in Ministère des Droits de la femme, *Dossier: Bilan* (1984).
50. See *Le Nouvel Observateur*, 25–31 July 1981. For an overview of the status of women in France and the accomplishments of the Ministère des Droits de la femme, see *Women of Europe*, no. 33 (15 November 1983–15 January 1984), pp. 28–30; and *Women of Europe*, no. 34 (15 January–15 March 1984), pp. 27–9.
51. *Citoyennes*, April 1983, pp. 9–11.
52. Ministère des Droits de la femme, Communiqué de presse, 16 July 1984 found in *Dossier: Loi sur l'égalité professionnelle* (1984).
53. *Le Monde*, 18 July 1984. (Emphasis added.)
54. 'Bilan des actions du Ministère des Droits de la femme, May 1981–March 1984', Ministère des Droits de la femme, *Dossier: Bilan* (1984).

55. Discours de Madame Roudy, 16 July 1984, in *Dossier: Loi sur l'égalité professionnelle* (1984).
56. *Citoyennes*, June 1984, p. 7.
57. Ibid.
58. Roudy, *La Femme en marge*, pp. 193–6.
59. See Jane Jenson, 'The Work of the Ministère des Droits de la femme', *Newsletter of the Conference Group on French Politics and Society*, no. 4 (December 1983), pp. 3–9.
60. Ozzello and Marks, 'Sous la rose', p. 218.
61. *Rapport au Ministre des Droits de la femme*, p. 76.
62. *Citoyennes*, January 1983, p. 14.
63. Ibid, November 1983, p. 7.
64. Interview with Catherine Beauvois (staff member of the Ministère des Droits de la femme), 20 July 1984. See also *Hommes et Libertés*, no. 33 (1984), pp. 8–12.
65. *Citoyennes*, June 1983, p. 9.
66. Ibid, p. 12.
67. See *Hommes et Libertés*, no. 33 (1984), p. 29.
68. *Citoyennes*, June 1983, p. 11.
69. Ibid.
70. See ibid, January 1983, p. 13.
71. Groult as quoted in *Médias et Langage*, no. 19–20 (1984), p. 26.
72. Discours de Madame Roudy, Séance plenière de la commission de terminologie, 26 April 1984, Ministère des Droits de la femme, *Dossier: Langage et terminologie concernant les activités des femmes* (1984).
73. See for example Benoîte Groult, 'Mme. le Secrétaire, Mme. le Ministre, Ça suffit ...', *Marie Claire*, March 1984, pp. 3–6.
74. *Citoyennes*, January 1983, p. 14. The Roudy ministry has also shown interest in trying to free prostitutes from dependence on male 'managers' and related problems faced by prostitutes in France.
75. Mossuz-Lavau and Sineau, *Enquête*, p. 12.
76. Ibid, pp. 11–12.
77. *Citoyennes*, May 1983, p. 9.
78. See for example Ministère des Droits de la femme, *Dossier: Les Femmes et l'Europe: Réunion informelle des ministres européens de l'emploi (1984)*.
79. *Le Monde*, 20 July 1984.
80. Jérôme Jaffré, *SOFRES, Opinion publique: enquêtes et commentaires 1984* (Paris: Gallimard, 1984), p. 38.
81. Ibid, p. 75.
82. Ibid, p. 19.
83. *Le Monde, Dossiers et documents: Les deuxièmes élections européennes, juin 1984* (Paris 1984), p. 69.
84. *Le Monde*, 26 June 1984.
85. See for example *Le Nouvel Observateur*, 22–28 June 1984, p. 25.
86. *Citoyennes*, February 1984, p. 11.

Party and Legislative Participation among Scandinavian Women

Ingunn Norderval

INTRODUCTION

According to E. E. Schattschneider, political parties have been the 'creators of democracy'.[1] In order to increase their bases of popular support, parties rather than public opinion demanded an extension of the franchise to working-class males, women, and ever younger age groups. Parties have thus played an important role in the integration of new groups within the political system.

In reference to women in particular, little is known about this integrative process. Party histories and documents generally neglect such questions as the recruitment of female members, women's mobility in party hierarchies, their contribution to policy development, and their public candidacy. Were women actively recruited as party members, or were they resented as intruders in an all-male political network? How did party women's associations develop, and what is their present role? How do formal and informal recruitment practices affect women and, finally, does women's presence in party organisations matter?

This article examines the impact of party and legislative participation upon women's political integration in the Scandinavian countries, which have earned a reputation as pioneers in the movement for women's rights. When Norway extended the suffrage to women on the same terms as men in 1913, it became the third nation in the world do do so; Finland had enfranchised women on the national level in 1906 but waited until 1917 to grant suffrage in local elections. In Denmark and Iceland, universal suffrage was granted in 1915, although in Iceland women and servants had to be 40 years old before they could vote. It was not until 1920 that Icelandic women could vote on the same terms as men, and not until 1921 that universal suffrage was adopted in Sweden.[2]

As shown in Table 1, fairly substantial proportions of contemporary political élites in all Scandinavian countries except Iceland are women. In 1984, women constituted between one-quarter and one-third of legislative assembly members and nearly the same fraction of cabinet ministers; women's representation in local and provincial politics as well as on committees, boards, and commissions has also increased markedly in recent years. Women's presence in the corporate channel has been especially notable in Norway, where 1973 government regulations helped to increase female membership on government-appointed boards. As well, recent changes in the equal status law demand that all public boards and committees must include members of both sexes, and that those with four or more members must include at least two appointees of each sex.[3]

TABLE 1

WOMEN IN SCANDINAVIAN PUBLIC OFFICE

	Local council(%)	Provincial council(%)	National Parliament(%)	Cabinet (prop.)	%
Denmark	21	20	26	5/21	23
Finland	22		31	3/17	18
Iceland	12		15	1/10	10
Norway	24	33	26	4/18	22
Sweden	29	31	28	5/19	26

Sources: Official election statistics and Torild Skard, 'Women in the political life of the Nordic countries', *International Social Science Journal* 35:4 (1983), p. 644.

Parties are key players in these efforts to improve female representation in both appointive and elective office in Sandinavia. Since candidates for such positions are normally selected on the basis of faithful service for some time in the party rank and file, the composition of government bodies is best understood with reference to party politics. To assess female representation in public life, then, we must consider the role of parties as 'creators of democracy' which, in the words of one Norwegian political scientist, have aided women in their transition from 'powerlessness without participation and representation whatsoever, to relative powerlessness in spite of participation'.[4]

SCANDINAVIAN PARTY SYSTEMS

Social scientists have proposed a five-party model of the Scandinavian political spectrum: on the far left, a communist or radical socialist party; towards the centre-left, a more moderate social democratic party; in the centre, a liberal and a farmers' party; and on the right, a conservative party. The closest approximation to this model is the Swedish case, where only five parties normally gain seats in the national legislature (*Riksdag*), followed by the Icelandic system, where four parties won seats in the *Alting* until a women's party gained over five per cent of the vote in 1983. By way of contrast, seven parties are currently represented in the Norwegian *Storting*, nine in the Danish *Folketing*, and nine in the Finnish *Eduskunta*.[5]

Although important cross-national differences thus characterise Scandinavian party politics, one generalisation which does hold concerns the increasingly weak position of liberal parties. None is at present represented in the legislatures of either Finland or Iceland, and in the other three cases liberal parties received less than six per cent of the vote in recent parliamentary elections. Some liberal support has been won by post-war Christian Democratic parties, particularly in Norway where the Christian People's Party is the third largest with about 10 per cent of the popular vote. In

Iceland, the largest parties in terms of electoral support are the (left) People's Alliance and Conservative parties, while in Norway, Sweden, Finland and Denmark, the largest are social democratic and conservative parties.[6]

PATTERNS OF PARTY SUPPORT

TABLE 2
FEMALE PARTY MEMBERS AND OFFICERS (%), 1980–82

	Party Members	Party Conference	National Council	Executive Council	Working Committee
Iceland					
People's Alliance		42	52	36	
Social Democrats		25	22	27	
Progress		21	14	14	
Independence		19	17	20	
Norway					
Communist	20–25	20	17	13	
Socialist Left	40	48	41	47	43
Labour	40	38	45	40	33
Liberal	42	41	46	56	
Center	33	33	36	45	25
Christian Peoples	55	32	27	45	40
Liberal Peoples	33	34	36	29	
Conservative	40–45	30		19	40
Progress				14	
Sweden					
Communist	38	36		34	29
Social Democrat	30	34		30	30
Liberal	45	43		44	38
Centre	8	32	29	24	29
Conservative	41	35	23	30	25
Denmark					
Communist	39	35		16	13
Left socialist	52	30		33	25
Socialist peoples	40	32		31	40
Social democrat		18		19	27
Radical liberal		40		23	27
Centre democrat	44	33			
Christian peoples	50	19		22	
Liberal	47	42		19	20
Conservative	30	30	28	18	
Progress		25		20	
Finland					
Communist	29	17		16	36
Democratic Alliance	32	31	22	25	33
Social Democrats	36	25	28	26	17
Liberal Peoples	55	45	35	30	33
Centre	38	25	28	16	25
Rural	19			10	
Christian Alliance	59	32	27	26	14
Swedish Peoples	35	33	27	28	27
National Alliance	50	36	25	24	17

Sources: Haavio-Mannila, *Det uferdige demokratiet*, pp. 67–68; and estimates by party headquarters of membership.

Gender differences in attitudes towards and membership in Scandinavian political parties have generally been slight. Although membership data are difficult to document – primarily because most parties do not retain separate male and female registration lists – figures which are available suggest that support for the various Scandinavian parties has been approximately the same for both men and women.[7] As reported in Table 2, women are estimated to constitute between 30 and 40 per cent of most party memberships,[8] the main exception being Christian people's parties which have 50 per cent or higher female memberships as well as majority female electoral bases. This exception parallels older comparative research on women's support for rightist and especially confessional political parties, which attributed such patterns to greater female religiosity, lower educational attainment, and the absence of radicalising influences in the workplace (notably trade unions).[9]

As women's educational and occupational status changes, however, the tendency toward female conservatism might be expected to weaken. Women presently constitute nearly one-half of the Scandinavian labour force, including 42, 44, and 45 per cent of the occupationally active populations in Norway, Denmark, and Sweden respectively. The most dramatic increase in female labour force participation has occurred among married women and young mothers; in Norway, for example, over 60 per cent of married women worked in 1984, compared with only nine per cent in 1960. More than half of Norwegian women with children under the age of seven are occupationally active.[10]

This growth in paid work, however, has been accompanied by a ghettoisation of women in low-paid part-time jobs, despite the presence of equal pay legislation. Female workers are also adversely affected by an acute shortage of both child-care facilities and public institutions for the sick and elderly. These conditions could be expected to contribute to increased support among women voters for parties of the left, a pattern which is reflected in Danish, Norwegian, and Swedish survey results. According to figures in Dahlerup (1979), women have constituted roughly 55 per cent of the electoral base of the Danish Social Democratic party in recent elections, at the same time as far right (Progress) parties in both Denmark and Norway have received disproportionate support from young men and very little among young women.[11] Scandinavian women have also been found to hold more pro-environmental attitudes than men, as reflected in the ability of the Swedish Centre party to win more support from women than from men in the 1979 elections – when the party strongly opposed nuclear power development.[12]

Although the evidence remains tentative, then, it would appear that contemporary patterns of party support in Scandinavia reflect some 'gender gap' trends. Women in general are more concerned than men with peace and environmental issues, while at the same time younger women vote left more than younger men, whose support for parties of the extreme right has grown.

ORGANISING WOMEN'S PARTIES

During the first two decades of this century, three basic strategies were available to women as they acquired formal political rights: first, to establish their own separate women's parties, independent of established groupings; second, to join existing political parties but form separate women's groups within them; and third, to work individually within established parties. The first option has captured the imagination of some women who believe that their collective interests are not sufficiently represented by existing parties and wish independent parties to challenge the larger ones to better articulate women's interests. Scandinavian women's parties have thus appeared from time to time as a reflection of frustration with existing party systems and women's inability to obtain influence within them, but also, paradoxically, as a reaction against what some perceived as the sordid, corrupt world of partisan politics. According to a 1901 statement by leading Norwegian suffragists, 'The main thing now is to work, not for a party but for a cause, in freedom and with responsibility. In practice, we must try to get rid of parties'.[13] Such opposition to party politics at times resulted in separate women's election lists and the organisations behind them becoming parties in all but name.

The independent party or election list strategy pursued by Scandinavian women has proved difficult to implement, despite its attractiveness to some feminists. Notably, experience in this region and elsewhere has shown that gender is a secondary type of political cleavage, and that women are as divided as men by primary class, ideological and cultural identifications.

Perhaps the best-known case of separate women's lists and (since 1983) a women's party can be found in Iceland, where various women's clubs sponsored successful election lists in municipal contests as early as 1908. National women's lists were organised in 1922 and 1926; notably, the list won 23 per cent of the vote and one seat in the former elections, but only 3.5 per cent and no seats in the latter. No further lists were attempted until 1982, when they appeared in a number of towns including Reykjavik and Akureiri. These successful efforts contributed to the formation of a women's party which contested the 1983 national elections, and won 5.5 per cent of the popular vote and five per cent of the legislative seats.[14]

In the light of the more limited success of independent lists and parties elsewhere, what factors explain the Icelandic experience? According to Styrkarsdottir (1981), early women's lists in Iceland benefited from a fluid social and political context through the first three decades of this century; Iceland was an agricultural society undergoing industrialisation, but political parties had not yet cemented their support bases within the new social groups thus created. During this transitional period, the absence of firm political loyalties worked in favour of women's lists, but the 'freezing' of the party system meant that by the late 1920s 'the women and their followers went over' to what became the established political organisations.[15]

Between 1930 and 1980, very few women (and, for long period, no women) were elected to the Alting. Frustration with this lack of electoral success through the established parties led activists in the contemporary women's movement to revive local lists in 1982 and to establish a women's party in 1983. This party competed in the 1983 general elections in Iceland; it won five per cent of the popular vote, seemed to encourage other parties to include more women on their lists, and helped female membership in the Alting to reach 15 per cent. Yet even this level remains relatively weak by Scandinavian standards, in large part because Iceland maintained a single-member plurality (as opposed to proportional representation) electoral system until 1959.[16] The 1959 adoption of proportionality, which has been shown to be more favourable to women than majoritarian arrangements, has only aided women marginally because the small size of the Alting (60 seats) and large number of parties fielding candidates in each electoral district mean that most parties can only hope to elect one member, usually a man. The new women's party was thus a response to Iceland's continued display of one common characteristic of single-member district arrangements, namely, few women in elective office at the national level.

Women's lists have also been attempted elsewhere in Scandinavia, including in Denmark where 13 and 11 per cent respectively of the women elected in 1909 and 1913 municipal elections won office through this route. Although all subsequent local elections in Denmark have featured women's lists, this strategy has played a relatively insignificant role in terms of overall numbers of women elected.[17] In Sweden, women's lists and parties have appeared sporadically since 1924, when the Liberal Party neglected demands for female representation. In 1927 and 1928, women's lists were entered in Swedish elections, but their limited appeal led activists to focus future efforts within the established parties.[18]

TABLE 3
WOMEN IN THE SCANDINAVIAN PARLIAMENTS (%)

	1918	1920	1929	1939	1949	1958	1966	1977	1984
Denmark	3	2	3	2	9	8	11	17	26
Finland	9	10	8	8	12	14	17	23	31
Iceland	0	0	3	2	4	2	2	5	15
Norway	0	1	1	1	5	7	8	24	26
Sweden	0	2	1	4	10	13	13	21	28

Source: Haavio-Mannila *et al.*, *Det uferdige demokratiet*, p. 91.

In Finland, women discussed the idea of a separate party at the time of their enfranchisement in 1906, but the idea did not catch on – largely because several women were nominated and elected by the established parties in these early years. As reflected in data in Table 3, Finland was considerably ahead of its neighbours in this respect, a trend which Haavio-Mannila (1981) attributes to simultaneous male and female enfranchisement in 1906.[19] Finnish men therefore had neither more experience than women nor an historical monopoly on political positions.

By way of contrast, 'non-political' women's lists appeared in Norway during the first election in which females could participate. Oslo suffragists thus urged newly enfranchised voters in 1901 'to think twice before attaching themselves to any political party ... if we hope to achieve anything and get any influence in society, women have to join forces'.[20] The major Norwegian parties strongly opposed separate lists, which were viewed as unwelcome and, in the case of the socialists, misleading electoral competitors. The Labour Party newspaper, *Socialdemokraten*, harshly criticised women's lists as merely an expression of upper-class interests which must be rejected by the working-class: 'It would be against all human sense of justice merely to think that working-class women in an election, where their most precious interests are at stake, should give these up and join the ranks of the reactionaries'.[21]

Separate lists in Norway were in fact quite unsuccessful among both working-class and middle-class women. The former were persuaded by Labour arguments concerning the need for class unity in the face of efforts by middle-class, conservative women to organise separate lists. Notably, the conservatives opposed extending the franchise to domestic servants, one of the largest groups of employed women.[22] Similarly, middle-class females generally rejected the idea of separate lists, but urged instead that pressure for increased nominations of women be exerted on established parties. The Norwegian Suffrage Association thus requested in 1901 that party organisations 'nominate a reasonable number of women on [their] lists in the autumn elections'.[23] This strategy, combined with active opposition to separate women's lists by the Labour Party, meant that efforts to sponsor women's lists or parties in Norway were rather unsuccessful during the early years of this century. Nor have they fared much better in recent years, since women's lists entered in the 1973 national legislative elections received less than 2,000 votes in total.[24]

PARTY WOMEN'S ORGANISATIONS

A second approach which has been pursued by politically active women in Scandinavia involves the establishment of organisations within the parties – an effort which has been attempted in some form in most party groupings. Although newer parties including the Socialist Left (Norway) and Socialist People's (Denmark) initially argued that women's organisations were anachronistic because women members should share the same rights and duties as men in the party, each eventually established a women's committee to formulate policy on women's issues, to hold women's conferences, etc. As well, the Danish Social Democratic Party – which disbanded its older women's organisation in 1969 in the name of equality – later established such a committee.

Before the establishment of newer, and seemingly more feminist, party women's committees, older party women's groups developed according to two distinctive models. One type, the double membership model, made female party members automatically members of the women's group and has been employed in the Norwegian Labour and, until 1969, Danish Social Democratic parties. Some observers maintain that this arrangement reflects a sceptical attitude towards factionalism among socialist party élites.[25] Given that neither Swedish nor Finnish Social Democrats employ the double membership model, and that the first Norwegian Labour women's group was formed with the blessings of the party leadership,[26] it is difficult to maintain that socialist ideology dictates this model.

Scandinavian organisations on the left, as well as the centre and right, have also established a second type of party women's group, which maintains separate (rather than double) membership lists, but remains affiliated with a larger party. Like the double-membership type, this second variety has assisted party campaign efforts, raised funds, and secured some influence for women in party politics.

The extent to which women have achieved influence through the party organisation route is questionable, however. As a Norwegian Labour leader, Martha Tynaes, observed in 1899, male party colleagues showed little understanding of women's weak position in the party and 'simply shrug their shoulders and usually ridicule our efforts'.[27] Tynaes therefore established a new Labour women's organisation in 1901, dedicated to 'gathering female union and workers' societies in our country in an association on a socialist foundation in order to protect their political interests'.[28] Like the older party women's group founded in 1895, though, this presumably more self-directed organisation worked for Labour in election campaigns and became an additional party wing among working-class women.

To what extent do party women's organisations inform and mobilise female voters, teach political skills, work for women's interests, and train candidates for party and public office? Some are ridiculed as ladies' sewing circles and coffee clubs which neither inform nor integrate women in the political system, and hardly threaten male élites in the larger party organisation. Women's associations have thus been described by their detractors as politically marginal, isolated and insignificant in terms of both party policy and the recruitment of female élites.[29]

This negative perception led to two seemingly contradictory developments in Scandinavia during the past two decades. First, the widely-held view that party women's groups were moribund offered a strong impetus for their dissolution – in some cases with the approval of women's group leaders. As the leader of the Norwegian Labour women's organisation stated in 1970, when 200 of the organisation's constituent groups had already ceased operation, 'I regard it as one of my most important tasks to see to it that as many women's groups as possible are disbanded'.[30]

Second, and quite paradoxically, this trend was stopped by the new women's movement. Contemporary feminists argued in favour of special organisations which could articulate and press for women's demands, so that women's groups were established or re-activated with some frequency. Traditional party women's groups also received an infusion of new vigour at precisely the same time that they were expected to disappear, and instead became active forces for placing new issues on the political agenda. The Norwegian Labour Party women's organisation, for example, became an effective change agent on party policies related to foreign affairs, defence, health care, abortion and other issues. These changes in the focus and composition of party women's groups stemmed the tide towards dissolution and rendered premature accounts of their imminent demise. In the words of Dahlerup (1983), 'the parties' women's organisations have changed, and in this change one finds their future legitimacy'.[31]

INDIVIDUAL PARTY PARTICIPATION

The third option available to Scandinavian women at the point of formal enfranchisement was individual involvement in regular party organisations. This strategy was not widely pursued in the early decades of this century despite women's fair representation as party members and the absence of codes or rules prohibiting their participation. As one local Labour leader reflected on the Norwegian situation, 'It was unheard of for women to come to the meetings. If a woman had come to a meeting, she would not have been thrown out or anything, but it would have been regarded as unusual. The women had their own group, the women's organisation'. During the post-war decades, female involvement in regular party activities has increased, although women remain a political minority.

Explanations of their relative absence in party life (other than at the levels of basic membership and participation in women's organisations) have usually focused on supply-side problems. That is, women are claimed to have few of the educational, occupational, financial, organisational and political (especially interest and ambition) resources required for élite-level party work. Willy Martinussen (1977) thus argues, 'We are dealing here with a set of interacting factors which create a systematic political deprivation of women'.[32] Women are the politically poor.

Recent research has drawn attention toward demand factors as well as supply (or resource) ones. In the demand view, political structures are themselves a hindrance or constraint upon female participation, since men are the gatekeepers who define the rules of entry, screen the recruits and keep powerful women to a minimum in order to retain male control over a system with limited rewards. As Maurice Duverger noted in his 1955 report, 'to give a post to a woman is to deprive a man of it and, in these circumstances, the posts given to women are cut down to the minimum required for propaganda purposes'.[33]

Scandinavian writers have thus highlighted the origins of limited female involvement in parties and in the wider political system rather than simply in women – who are increasingly viewed as victims of both deliberate and unwitting oligarchy in party organisations. Sponsorship by a mentor is particularly important in Scandinavian politics, where self-recruitment has generally been seen as violating a fundamental cultural norm of modesty. Political hopefuls therefore depend upon political godparents to sponsor each career step; this process has thus far provided an enormous built-in advantage for men. Whether through unwitting processes whereby only the names of men are proposed, or through more conscious, deliberate acts which exclude women from visible positions that could later advance their political careers, party recruitment practices operate in a manner which is far from gender-neutral. Potential female élites thus require political mentors of their own, godmothers who can sponsor their careers behind the scenes and teach them how to outwit a system which has hitherto outwitted most women.

Recent changes in the broader recruitment system promise greater opportunity for Scandinavian women to break through gatekeeping obstacles. Feminist activists have pressured for an explicit recognition of the biases inherent in established recruitment practices, and have won support for numerical quota rules to ensure fairer representation. Quota-based reforms have been most widely accepted in Norway, where the Socialist Left, Labour, and Liberal Parties each require at least 40 per cent representation of each sex at all levels of party activity. In the Labour and Socialist Left Parties, this rule applies to candidacy for all elective offices, including safe positions on party lists.

The implications of these quota rules are important. First, at the level of party membership, organisations need to recruit women more actively. In the words of one Norwegian Labour official, 'We have over 3,000 local chapters, many of which have *almost only* male members. If they are going to fulfill the [quota] requirements, which they *must*, they simply have to recruit more women'.[34]

Second, quota rules have exerted a spillover or contagion effect from the left to parties of the centre and right. As reflected in Norwegian data in Table 2, female representation in most central party executives is quite high, in some cases higher than the corresponding percentage of female members. Perhaps most notable are central executive figures from the Christian People's and Centre Parties – both conservative groupings whose major base is among rural voters with traditional sex role orientations – which both show a level of 45 per cent female representation.

Third, the impact of quotas appears to be greatest in central as opposed to local party organisations, where it is commonly argued that women are reluctant to accept political positions. In the words of Norwegian cabinet minister Astrid Gjertsen, a Conservative:

> It is my impression that the parties at the local level are less conscious of equality issues than the central institutions. This indicates that the parties' own equality ideology, which dominates the party platforms, is not always taken seriously by the organisational apparatus and local party branches.[35]

This view is shared by a leader of the Centre Party: 'It seems that women prosper, relatively speaking, in those areas governed and controlled by the central party apparatus'.[36]

Although local leaders maintain that they are unable to meet quota requirements due to an absence of interested women, recent research suggests a somewhat different situation. According to Larsen and Offerdal (1979), a majority of both men and women in Norway are unwilling to hold any political position, but of those willing to serve, men are much more likely than women to be asked. Among the latter group, 37 per cent of men compared with only 21 per cent of women had been approached to serve.[37]

While quotas will compel parties to recruit female candidates, it is clear that many local organisations conduct this search half-heartedly and deliberately abandon their pursuit of women in the name of 'practical politics' and 'common sense'. None the less, the quota regulations have proved a useful tool for women, particularly on the national level of Norwegian politics. The completed round of nominations for the 1985 Storting elections, for example, indicates that over one-third of the new legislature, including about 45 per cent of the Labour members, will be female.

NATIONAL LEGISLATIVE OFFICE

The number and proportion of women in national legislative office in Scandinavia have attracted global attention, largely from scholars and activists who seek to understand why so many women – in relative terms – have won elective office in this region. We shall consider this question first with reference to the prevailing 'rules of the game' generally in electoral politics, and will then focus on the specific case of the Norwegian Labour Party, where the author has been active as an elected legislator at the provincial level.

TABLE 4
FEMALE CANDIDATES ON PARLIAMENTARY PARTY LISTS[a]

	Denmark	Finland	Iceland[b]	Norway
1917-18	9	11	--	2
1920-22	4	8	--	4
1929-30	3	8	--	7
1936-39	4	9	--	10
1947-49	11	12	--	16
1960-62	12	15	--	19
1969-71	16	21	--	20
1977-79	22	26	25	32
1981-83	25	29	35	37

a Cell entries represent percentages. Since elections are not held the same years, or with the same frequency in each country, it is necessary to look at the lists during a period rather than in a single year.
b No complete statistics are available for Sweden, or for Iceland before 1974. It is estimated that females were 15–18 per cent of Swedish list candidates in 1952.

All the Scandinavian systems are parliamentary democracies, where legislators are selected in multi-member districts on the basis of proportional representation (PR). Since parties are crucial to the formation of lists or slates under PR, the increase in female candidacies during the last two decades, as reported in Table 4, has had a direct impact on women's legislative representation. From a level of 10 per cent or fewer female list candidacies as recently as the inter-war period, their proportion has increased to approximately 25 per cent in Denmark and Finland and over 33 per cent in Norway and Iceland.

The basic impact of PR systems upon female representation is complicated by the presence of rank-ordering arrangements in Norway, Sweden, and Iceland, compared with preferential voting systems in Denmark and Finland. In the case of rank-ordering, candidates' chances of election are strictly dependent upon their place in the party list, whether at the top in party-held (or safe) positions, farther down in challenger posts, or in the lowest level 'frill' positions. Women have in the past been disproportionately clustered in lower list slots in rank-ordered systems and, as a result, they have had limited chances for election in the relatively stable party environments of Iceland, Norway, and Sweden. Indeed, since it is quite rare for a party to gain more than one new seat in any electoral district, the second position beneath the last seat held is for all practical purposes a write-off, and research shows women to be far more numerous in such challenger and frill positions than in safe slots. By way of contrast, preferential balloting arrangements permit voters to reorder their party lists by casting personal votes for any list candidate. This system has proved far more favourable to female legislative representation than the rank-ordering approach.

How do candidates obtain a list nomination, and what factors contribute to 'safe' list positions? In the Norwegian case, which is useful for illustrative purposes, *Storting* candidates are selected by provincial party nominating conventions after names have been proposed by the nominating committee. The composition of the nominating committee is thus of crucial importance to political hopefuls. Formally, it is the party conference which selects the committee on the recommendation of the party executive. In practice, however, a party secretary may wield considerable power and get his suggestions regarding the composition of the nominating committee adopted without change by the party executive and in turn ratified by the party conference. The party conference is itself free to change the list, but once again the force inherent in an executive committee proposal is often so strong as to overwhelm challenges to the official choice.

The 'trial nominations' constitute the next stage. The nominating committee solicits names from the local party organisations for possible inclusion on the list. At the local level, the trial nominations usually elicit only slight interest. They tend to be dominated by local party élites who suggest their favourite candidates to the committee. On the basis of all suggestions received, committee members compose an initial list. Incumbents seeking re-election are usually ranked at the top, so that the many local party proposals are relevant only for lower 'frill' positions. Party élites seek to balance their list by representing all major geographical areas, trade unions in the case of socialist parties, youth, women, and various occupational groupings. In the ensuing juggling act, many good candidates may be dropped from consideration because they do not meet the various balancing criteria. Local party reaction to this first list is generally limited. Few people attend meetings where it is debated, and the contests which do develop are largely played out in inner élite circles. Not surprisingly, the final list proposed by the nominating committee is often identical to the initial one.

More eventful, and potentially dramatic, developments may occur as a result of the retirement of, or widespread disapproval with, an incumbent. Such situations may provide an opportunity for broader democratic input into party nominations and may thus revitalise the political process. But even then, the advantage usually rests with the party élite which, if it supports a candidate, knows how to quell opposition. One recent example from Norway is relevant. Dissatisfaction had grown within one of the provincial parties with an incumbent who was seeking re-nomination. Support for a rival candidate was mobilised, and there were efforts to 'pack' local meetings where delegates to the nominating convention were elected. If such 'coups' are successful in a number of municipalities, they may later cause dramatic confrontations and unexpected results at the provincial nominating convention, the decisions of which are final and binding upon the party.

In this particular case, however, rumours of the local 'coup' reached supporters of the incumbent in the party secretariat, who then called home the representative from Oslo to appear at the meeting where delegates to the nominating convention were elected. Party insiders also packed the hall with supporters – a strategy which, combined with the psychologically devastating presence of the incumbent, ensured local support for renomination. In this manner, the party élite successfully quelled dissent by imposing strict discipline through the mobilisation of local 'old guard' delegates to a nominating meeting. Michels' famous dictum, 'Who says organisation says oligarchy', thus operated at each stage of the list-building process. The organisational advantage remained in the hands of élite insiders, who identified and controlled a rebellion with relative ease using their skill and position in the party hierarchy.

What factors help women to secure 'safe' nominations? Research by Skard and others suggests that female chances increase with the number of seats held by a provincial party. In the 1981 Norwegian election, women obtained 16 per cent of safe positions in parties electing one or two legislators, compared with 35 per cent in those electing more than two members.[38] This result confirms earlier findings which show that the two largest parties in the *Storting*, Labour and Conservative, have elected most of the women who have served as legislators.

Similarly, recent research in Sweden indicates that only eight per cent of the legislators elected by small parties (defined as those holding a single seat) were female, while 29 per cent of those from parties with more than one seat were women. In Iceland as well, data from 1979 elections to the Alting show that all three women elected in that year represented parties holding three or more seats.[39]

Party size is only one factor affecting safe nominations, however. Smaller parties of the left may also ensure female representation at the top of their lists because of a commitment to egalitarian ideology, as reflected in the Norwegian Socialist Left case. The latter elected four members to the *Storting* in the most recent elections, the same as the right-wing Progress Party; notably, while the Socialist Left has two female representatives, Progress has none.

Finally, a realistic assessment of the candidate-choosing process would seem to aid women's chances for safe nomination. At each stage of the process, party insiders (generally men) are in control, so that women are disadvantaged by both their smaller numbers and relative political inexperience. As well, feminists are particularly limited by their ideological commitment to more open and democratic political participation, which makes many averse to playing the game of politics by established patriarchal rules. The price thus paid for such idealism amounts to inefficiency and impotence in party matters.

The feminist dilemma, then, in seeking to obtain greater policy and especially legislative influence is that in order to change party structures, one must implicitly accept these structures and relevant 'rules of the game'. The risk for activists within the system remains that by the time they obtain sufficient power to effect change, they no longer see the need for reform. Many feminists have feared precisely this contradiction and have rejected party politics, while others have remained optimists within the system, believing that party democracy is strengthened through their internal efforts.

POLICY IMPACT

Attempts to improve women's representation in legislative and party office ultimately confront the question, 'So what? Does women's presence in politics really matter?' Scandinavian arguments for increased numbers of females generally rely upon three principles: First, democratic justice; second, resource utilisation; and third, interest representation.[40] According to the first point, since women constitute roughly half the population, they are entitled to comparable numerical representation in those bodies which determine the laws under which they must live. The second position suggests that valuable human resources are wasted when women are not involved in politics; in this view, no society can afford to leave untapped half of its available talent.

According to the third principle, which is increasingly popular in Scandinavia and elsewhere, women and men have different political interests because of gender-based differentiations throughout the social structure. Female exclusion from or under-representation in political activities therefore means that women's interests are poorly represented. Implicit in this third position is the assumption that women in politics do, or would, pursue different issues from men.

A series of recent studies conducted in Finland, Norway, and Sweden tend to confirm this assumption. According to Skard (1980), Sinkkonen and

TABLE 5

FEMALE MEMBERSHIP IN PARLIAMENTARY COMMITTEES (%) 1981–85

Committee Jurisdiction	Denmark	Finland	Iceland	Norway	Sweden
Social welfare	47	41	14	50	47
Education, church, culture	40	47	14	46	37
Consumer affairs, administration				50	
Local affairs, labor, housing	24			38	33
Foreign affairs	24	18		25	27
Constitutional affairs, justice	36	43	14	28	24
Transport, traffic	6	12		31	13
Agriculture, fisheries, forestry		18		17	13
Energy/industry	24			7	13
Finance, economics, taxation	12	31		17	7
Defence	12	18		10	13
Others		44	14		
Women in Parliament (%)	24	31	5	28	28
Size of Parliament (Total N)	179	200	60	155	349

Source: Haavio-Mannila et al., *Det uferdige demokratiet*, p. 97.

Haavio-Mannila (1981) and other sources, female legislators indeed have different priorities from men, since the former generally focus upon issues which represent extensions of the conventional feminine sphere – notably health, education, child care, family law and social welfare defined more generally. In the words of Liljestrom and Dahlstrom (1981), political women concentrate on 'the sphere of reproduction', and men on 'the sphere of production', where the latter includes such areas as finance, taxation, energy, communication, and the system-maintenance areas of foreign policy, defence and justice.[41]

These differences in policy focus are evident in the committee assignments of female legislators (see Table 5) and in regular parliamentary debates, where it is generally women members who pursue issues of specific relevance to women. Analyses of the questions and motions submitted before the Norwegian *Storting* in 1973–77 show that 20 per cent of female members' interventions could be classified as pertaining to women's interests, compared with only four per cent of those made by men. In Finland, comparable figures for female and male legislators were 10 against one per cent, and in Sweden, nine against two per cent.[42]

Overall, then, it would appear that many women in public office feel a special obligation to represent women as a group. Their ability to do so is limited, however, by the fact that female legislators have little control over either committee or party leadership positions, and thus over the larger parliamentary agenda.[43] Women are thus less likely to participate in debates because they remain clustered in lower status committees and, more specifically, in assignments which represent an extension of older domestic roles. Exceptions to this pattern have occurred, though, following the selection of women as parliamentary party leaders by the Social Democrats of Denmark, Norway and Sweden; the Socialist Left Party of Norway; the Socialist People's Party of Denmark; the Communist Party of Finland; the People's Democrats of Finland; and, of course, the Women's Party of Iceland. Given that several other parties of the centre and right have also chosen women as deputy parliamentary leaders in recent years, the prospects for improving representation in parliamentary politics seem hopeful.

CONCLUSION

This article began by questioning the role of Nordic political parties as 'creators of democracy', particularly their success in integrating women during the decades since formal enfranchisement. Our discussion suggests that the record of the parties is mixed; although female suffrage was enacted, political organisations were reluctant to recruit new voters as activists and legislative candidates. Only with the growth of the contemporary feminist movement, when women began to demand greater numerical and policy representation in parties, did parties respond through the adoption of formal quota rules and informal efforts to recruit female members, officers and candidates.

Despite these apparent signs of progress, however, many female party activists remain frustrated with their status at the same time as some men have become increasingly resentful of what they perceive as feminist intrusions within party organisations. Much of this tension is palpable although difficult to measure; that is, women believe that men are often inattentive, ridiculing, and unwilling to consider women and women's issues in serious debate. The recent wave of political and social conservatism has clearly fuelled male chauvinism within the parties, as reflected in open criticism of quota rules and use of the term 'feminist' as an epithet in debates. As Norwegian legislator Sissel Ronbeck observed,

> You know you get a minus in the ledger. You know you have the choice, whether to talk about women's issues or be heard. But if you talk about the *budget balance* and *about the relationship between the*

deficit and the GNP ... then you are with it. Then you have understood.[44]

A sense of frustration, disillusionment, and frequently betrayal has therefore at times clouded women's recent experiences in party politics, which in turn encourage a withdrawal from party organisations and a strengthening of popular stereotypes about lack of interest in politics among women.

There is one type of political activity where women participate as much as men, however: ad hoc issue coalitions. According to Hernes and Voje (1980), 'women come into their own in this type of [ad hoc] activity', primarily because issue coalitions are less demanding of time and energy in the long term, and less plagued by organisational 'bottlenecks' than established parties.[45] Women's roles in a sex-differentiated society have encouraged them to develop practical problem-solving skills, in some cases through the expansion of neighbourhood networks into ad hoc issue movements.[46]

The Scandinavian peace movement offers a useful illustration of the possibilities of ad hoc politics, at the same time as it reflects the inherent limitations of this approach. Ad hoc action may be a useful way to attract attention to new issues, but it is the quiet, persistent work through regular political channels which is necessary to solve most problems. In the long run, then, the full political integration and representation of women depends upon parties' assuming a more active and aggressive role as the 'creators of democracy' than they have done so far.

NOTES

1. E. E. Schattschneider, *Party Government* (New York, 1942), p. 1.
2. See E. Haavio-Mannila *et al.* (eds.), *Det uferdige demokratiet* (Oslo: 1983), pp. 58–62 for a discussion of the introduction of suffrage in the Scandinavian countries.
3. Equal Status Law, paragraph 21, in *Likestillingspolitikk* (Oslo: Department of Consumer Affairs and Government Administration, 1982), p. 64.
4. Haavio-Mannila, *Det uferdige*, p. 4. Translations from this and other sources are by the author.
5. For a discussion of Scandinavian party systems, see Olof Petersson, *Folkstyrelse och statsmakt i Norden* (Uppsala: Diskurs, 1984), Ch. 4; and Erik Allardt *et al.*, *Nordic Democracy* (Copenhagen: Det Danske Selskab, 1981), Ch. 4.
6. Petersson, *Folkstyrelse*, p. 51.
7. Drude Dahlerup, 'Udviklingslinier i Kvinders politiske deltagelse og repraesentation i Danmark', in Mogens N. Pedersen (ed.), *Dansk politik i 1970'erne* (Samfundsvidenskabeligt Forlag, 1979), p. 121, reports that female membership in the Danish Social Democratic Party increased from 17 per cent in 1915 to 40 per cent at its peak in the 1950s.
8. Petersson, *Folkstyrelse*, p. 60; Haavio-Mannila, *Det uferdige*, p. 66; and Torild Skard, 'Women in the political life of the Nordic countries', *International Social Science Journal*, 35:4 (1983), pp. 646–9.
9. See, for example, Maurice Duverger, *The Political Role of Women* (Paris: UNESCO, 1955) and Harriet Holter, *Sex Roles and Social Structure* (Oslo: Universitetsforlaget, 1970).
10. See *Tjenestemannsbladet*, No. 6, (August–September 1984), p. 1.
11. Dahlerup, 'Udviklingslinier', p. 125; and Henry Valen, *Valg og politikk* (Oslo: NKS-Forlaget, 1981), p. 379.
12. Petersson, *Folkstyrelse*, pp. 60–67.

13. Anne Loennechen, 'Kvinners Kommunepolitiske Aktivitet i Kristiania fra 1901 til 1907', M.A. thesis, University of Bergen, 1983, p. 21.
14. See Audur Styrkarsdottir, 'Om kvindernes muligheder for opstilling til valg i V-Europa?', paper presented at Nordisk Ministerråds konference om Kvinder i Styrende Organer, Copenhagen, October 1981.
15. Ibid, p. 3.
16. Numerous studies have shown that electoral systems featuring proportional representation are more favourable to women than single-member district systems. See Wilma Rule, 'Why Women Don't Run: The Critical Contextual Factors in Women's Legislative Recruitment', *Western Political Quarterly* 34:1 (1981), pp. 60–77; Ingunn Norderval Means, 'Political Recruitment of Women in Norway', *Western Political Quarterly* 25:3 (1972), pp. 491–521; Duverger, *Political Role*, pp. 80, 88; and Torild Skard, *Utvalgt til Stortinget* (Oslo: Gyldendal, 1980), pp. 42–64.
17. Haavio-Mannila, *Det uferdige*, p. 73.
18. Ibid, p. 72.
19. Elina Haavio-Mannila, 'Kvinnor i styrande organ i Finland', paper delivered at Nordisk Ministerråd's conference, Copenhagen, October 1981, p. 1.
20. Loennechen, 'Kvinners', p. 15.
21. Quotation reported in ibid, p. 26.
22. Ibid, pp. 18–20, 106–110.
23. Ibid, p. 17.
24. See Norderval Means, 'Political Recruitment', p. 519; and Haavio-Mannila, *Det uferdige*, p. 72.
25. Dahlerup, 'Udviklingslinier', pp. 118–119; and Haavio-Mannila, *Det uferdige*, p. 29.
26. Loennechen, 'Kvinners', p. 96.
27. Ibid, p. 98.
28. Ibid.
29. Henry Valen speculated in an early article that a relationship existed between the size of women's auxiliaries and female political representation. See his 'Recruitment of Parliamentary Nominees in Norway', *Scandinavian Political Studies* 1 (1966), p. 133. The case of the Centre parties clearly weakens this hypothesis: with the strongest or one of the strongest women's auxiliaries in several Scandinavian countries, they elected very few female legislators until the Swedish Centre Party in the 1970s attracted female support for its stand on nuclear energy, and elected a fairly high proportion of women (23 per cent) to the *Riksdag*.
30. Interview with Sonja Ludvigsen, leader of the Norwegian Labour Party women's organisation, 1970.
31. Drude Dahlerup, 'Kvindeorganisationerne i Norden: Afmagt eller Modmagt?' in *Det uferdige*, p. 36.
32. Willy Martinussen, *The Distant Democracy*, (London: Wiley, 1977), p. 200.
33. Duverger, *The Political Role*, p. 125.
34. Likestillingsutvalget, *Rapport fra kontaktkonferansen med organisasjonene*, (Oslo: Likestillingsrådet, 1984), p. 116.
35. Ibid, p. 14.
36. Ibid, p. 122.
37. Stein Ugelvik Larsen and Audun Offerdal, *De få vi valgte* (Oslo: Universitetsforlaget, 1979), pp. 94–7.
38. Skard, 'Women'. For additional material on élite-level participation, see Torild Skard, 'Progress for Women: Increased Female Representation in Political Elites in Norway', in Cynthia Fuchs Epstein and Rose Laub Coser (eds.), *Access to Power* (London: Allen & Unwin, 1981), pp. 76–89; Elina Haavio-Mannila, 'Sex Roles in Politics', in Constantina Safilios-Rothschild (ed.), *Toward a Sociology of Women* (Toronto: Xerox College Publishing, 1972), pp. 154–72; Ingunn Norderval Means, 'Women in Local Politics: The Norwegian Experience', *Canadian Journal of Political Science* 5:3 (1972), 365–88 and 'Scandinavian Women', in Lynn E. Iglitzin and Ruth Ross (eds.), *Women in the World* (Santa Barbara: Clio Books, 1976).
39. Haavio-Mannila, *Det uferdige*, pp. 85–6.
40. Helga Maria Hernes, *Staten – Kvinner ingen adgang* (Oslo: Universitetsforlaget, 1982),

p. 81.
41. Rita Liljeström and Edmund Dahlström, *Arbetarkvinnor i hem – arbete och samhällsliv* (Jönköping: Tiden 1981), pp. 32–4. See also Christina Högberg, 'Kvinnors motioner i riksdagen', manuscript cited in Haavio-Mannila, *Det uferdige*, p. 109; Skard, *Utvalgt til Stortinget*, pp. 187–95; and Sirkka Sinkkonen and Elina Haavio-Mannila, 'The Impact of the Women's Movement and Legislative Activity of Women MPs on Social Development', in Margherita Rendel (ed.), *Women, Power and Political Systems* (London: Croom Helm, 1981), pp. 195–215.
42. Haavio-Mannila, *Det uferdige*, p. 111.
43. Ottar Hellevik, *Stortinget – en sosial elite?* (Oslo: Pax, 1969), Ch. 10–12, and Skard, *Utvalgt til Stortinget*, Ch. 5.
44. Interview with Sissel Rønbeck in *Arbeiderungdommen* No. 9 (November 1984), p. 5. Italics in original.
45. Helga Marie Hernes and Kirsten Voje, 'Women in the Corporate Channel in Norway: A Process of Natural Exclusion?' *Scandinavian Political Studies* 3:2 (1980), p. 177.
46. Ibid, pp. 179–80.

Women's Legislative Participation in Western Europe

Pippa Norris

INTRODUCTION

One of the most reliable and widely accepted generalisations in political science is that in virtually every society the higher echelons of power are dominated by men.[1] Rule by men is so pervasive that writers refer to an 'iron law of andrarchy' in politics.[2] In some societies, however, this generalisation needs to be questioned. Over the years only a few women have been elected to the British Parliament, the US Congress and the French National Assembly, but in other societies, such as Finland, Denmark and the Netherlands, there have been remarkable changes during the last 20 years. Why do these differences exist, and what factors help to account for increased female representation? This article compares women legislators in developed liberal, and especially Western European, democracies, questioning whether cultural, socio-economic or institutional factors are most significant in explaining cross-national differences. Since in all 24 nations considered, women formally enjoy equal rights to compete for office, we ask, 'given legal equality, why are women more successful in gaining entry to parliamentary élites in some countries than others?'

LEGISLATIVE OFFICE

Although nowhere in Western Europe do women achieve equal legislative representation, there exist striking contrasts between countries. A relatively high proportion (15 to 31 per cent) hold national office in Sweden, Finland, Denmark, Norway, and the Netherlands (see Figure 1, Table 1). At a slightly lower level, we find that approximately 10 per cent of parliamentarians in Portugal, West Germany and Switzerland are women, while even fewer (< 5 per cent) hold office in Britain, Greece and Spain. Because these differences tend to exist at other, sub-national levels of government in each case, we would propose that where women are relatively numerous in national office, they are also likely to do well in local government, such that there is generally a strong association between representation at the two levels (r = .90).

In cross-national terms, results of the 1984 direct elections to the European Parliament permit us to compare candidates from a range of liberal democracies in simultaneous elections for the same office. Although there were national differences in the EEC campaigns (e.g., the electoral systems were not the same throughout the Community), the results allow more uniform comparisons for European countries than other data. As shown in Table 1, cross-cultural differences in the representation of women in local and national political élites continue at the level of the European Parlia-

WOMEN'S LEGISLATIVE PARTICIPATION IN EUROPE 91

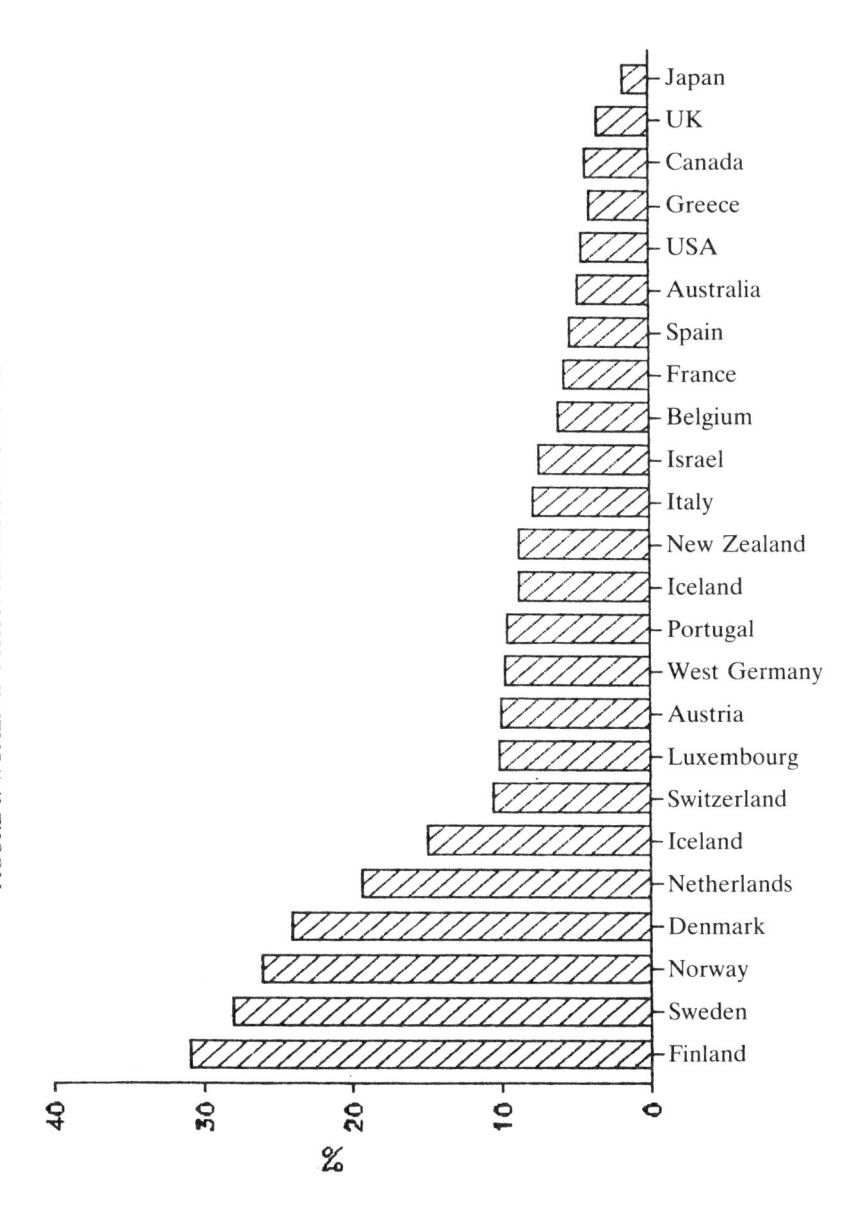

FIGURE 1: WOMEN IN NATIONAL LEGISLATURES 1983

TABLE 1
WOMEN IN EUROPEAN PUBLIC OFFICE, 1979-84 (%)

Country	Date	National Level Lower House	National Level Upper House	Cabinet	Local Level Regional	European Parliament City	1984
Finland	1983	31	n.r	18	–	22	n.r
Sweden	1983	28	n.r	26	31	29	n.r
Norway	1983	26	n.r	22	29	23	n.r
Denmark	1983	24	n.r	15	20	21	38
Netherlands	1984	19	19	12	16.5	13	28
Iceland	1983	15	n.r	10	–	12	n.r
Switzerland	1979	11	7	0	10	14	n.r
Luxembourg	1982	10	–	8	–	–	17
Austria	1981	10	21	26	21	11	n.r
West Germany	1983	10	5	6	8	2	20
Portugal	1982	10	–	8	–	–	n.r
Ireland	1983	9	10	8	5	20	13
New Zealand	1982	9	n.r	10	7	3	10
Italy	1983	8	4	0	4	–	n.r
Israel	1983	8	3	–	–	–	17
Belgium	1983	6	12	16	8	3	21
France	1982	6	3	11	14	8	n.r
Spain	1982	6	4	5	6	6	n.r
Australia	1983	5	19	–	7	10	n.r
USA	1984	5	2	16	13	–	n.r
Greece	1983	4	–	7	–	–	n.r
Canada	1984	4	–	7	8	18	n.r
UK	1983	4	7	9	16	2	15
Japan	1982	2	7	–	1		n.r
Average		13	9	11	14	13	20

Sources: *Women of Europe*; S. Bristow, 'Women Councillors; An Explanation of the Underrepresentation of Women in Local Government', *Local Government Studies* 6:3 (1980), pp. 73–90; Center for the American Woman and Politics, 'Women in Elective Office: Factsheet', 1984; C. Matsell, 'Spain', in Joni Lovenduski and Jill Hills (eds.), *The Politics of the Second Electorate* (London: Routledge & Kegan Paul, 1981); R. Walmsley, 'Women, Feminism and the Political Process', *Politics* 17:2 (1982), pp. 65–9; A. Smyth, 'Women and Power in Ireland', paper presented at Second International Congress on Women, Groningen, 1984; T. Skaard, 'Women in the Political Life of the Nordic Countries', *International Social Science Journal* 35:4 (1984), pp. 639–57; and T. Skaard, 'Progress for Women: Increased Female Representation in Political Elites in Norway', in C.F. Epstein and R.L. Coser (eds.), *Access to Power* (London: Allen & Unwin, 1981); UN Selected Statistics on the Status of Women (New York, 1985).

ment. Where women politicians are strongly represented nationally, such as in Denmark and the Netherlands, they have generally done well in the European Parliament, while the reverse is true in such countries as the United Kingdom and Italy. Overall, women are more strongly represented at the European level: in the 1984 elections, 75 women were elected out of 434 legislators, or 17 per cent of the total, which is double the percentage in equivalent national parliaments. This figure represents a considerable change since the first Common Assembly of the EEC (1952–58), when only one woman was nominated out of 78 members (1.3 per cent). Female representation increased marginally to 3 per cent by 1972 and 5.5 per cent by 1978, but only following the direct elections of 1979 did a substantial breakthrough occur.[3]

At the level of cabinet membership and government leadership, there have been so few women that we cannot reliably generalise. Those who have been elected to prime ministerial and presidential office in developed democracies include Margaret Thatcher in Britain, Golda Meir in Israel, and Gro Brundtland in Norway. With the possible exception of the latter, it cannot be said that women as a group have made important breakthroughs to power in these nations. Rather, particular *individuals* have used a combination of luck, talent and ability to take advantage of particular circumstances, leading to their *individual* rise to power.[4] In cabinet office, women have been relatively numerous in the Scandinavian countries; for example, in the 1980 Swedish government, five female members sat in a cabinet of 20 ministers (25 per cent).

Turning to trends over time, we find that differences between countries have generally increased since the 1960s (see Figure 2). The number of women in national office in such countries as Britain and the USA has remained fairly steady or even declined over the years, despite the common media impression of gradual progress. In fact, women in the British House of Commons in 1983 numbered 23 out of 650, or 3.5 per cent. By way of comparison, there has been continuous growth in the proportion of female legislators in Scandinavia and the Netherlands; as well, recent improvements have occurred in France, Switzerland, Ireland and Italy, although the extent of these changes should not be exaggerated. How do we explain why women politicians are getting on further and faster in some political systems than others?

INSTITUTIONAL, CULTURAL AND SOCIO-ECONOMIC EXPLANATIONS

Previous research suggests that institutional, cultural and socio-economic factors affect the position of women in political élites. Much comparative research has emphasised institutional influences, particularly the type of electoral system used in different countries. Many writers argue that proportional representation under a party list system offers women a much better chance for nomination and election than simple plurality systems.[5] This view is supported by evidence showing that countries with first-past-the-post systems, such as Britain and Canada, have only a handful of women in Parliament, while female representation is generally stronger in countries

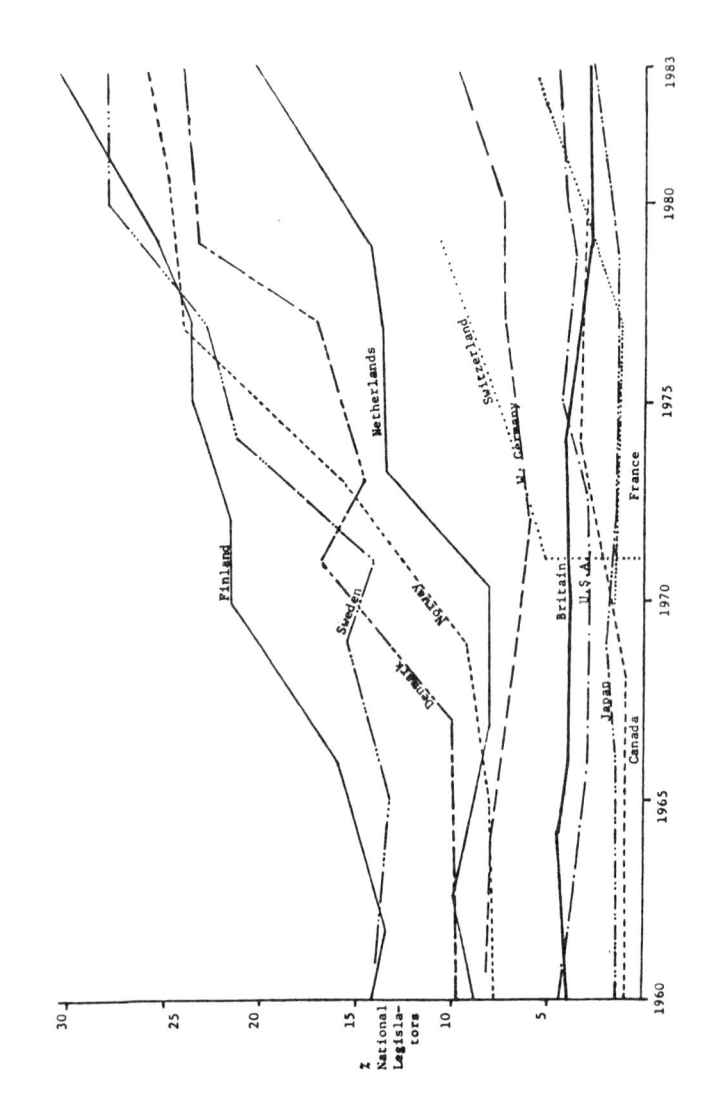

FIGURE 2: % FEMALE NATIONAL LEGISLATORS IN THE LOWER HOUSE: SELECTED COUNTRIES 1960–83

using proportional representation, such as Sweden and Norway. Yet it is unclear why there are significant differences between countries which share a similar electoral system such as Belgium and Denmark, or Italy and the Netherlands. It is also unclear how much the introduction of proportional representation, by itself, would improve the political position of women. These points suggest the need to analyse the relative influence of voting systems versus other factors, especially cultural ones, since elections operate within a broader societal context.

A number of existing studies maintain that cultural variations are equally, if not more, important than institutional factors. Women have been elected in the greatest numbers in Western countries sharing a Nordic heritage, while they have done relatively poorly in countries sharing Anglo-American traditions (notably Britain, the USA, Australia, Canada and New Zealand). Do Nordic cultures share a liberal attitude towards the role of women, while other societies hold more conservative and traditional values? Clearly, cultural views could play an important role in the three hurdles women have to cross to achieve elective office: that is, they must be willing to stand, must be judged suitable candidates by a party selectorate, and must be supported by the voters. If societal attitudes towards female élites are negative, then this factor could influence the numbers of women who want to stand for office, who believe that politics would be an appropriate vocation, and who think that they stand a chance of winning. Perceptions of women as vote-losers within a party selectorate mean that female electoral prospects would also be viewed as doubtful.[6] Lastly, public attitudes could be reflected directly in the votes which female candidates attract, since considerations of gender might override other factors such as partisanship.

A third set of studies emphasise socio-economic rather than cultural factors; in particular, these sources highlight the proportion of women who are eligible for public office by virtue of their economic and educational backgrounds. According to this view, party selection committees will nominate only those candidates who have certain qualifications, notably a college education. A number of studies demonstrate that university qualifications distinguish élites from non-élites throughout the world.[7] Compared with their proportion in the general population, university graduates are statistically over-represented in legislative élites roughly 10 or 20 to one.[8] Education also tends to motivate candidates to stand for election; studies report that people with higher education participate more than others in a variety of cultural milieux.[9] Educated citizens are more likely to follow current events in the media, to acquire information about government, to feel competent to discuss political issues and to be politically efficacious. As women obtain more formal education, they may therefore gain increased representation on élite levels.

Studies also suggest a significant connection between female political recruitment and patterns of employment. Political élites tend to be drawn from a small number of occupational groups, particularly the professions. Lawyers are politically prominent in many nations, comprising 15–50 per cent of national legislators.[10] Journalists, academics, teachers and businessmen are also statistically over-represented in parliaments.[11] These occupational backgrounds provide expertise and confidence in public speaking, knowledge of government and familiarity with the law, as well as considerable flexibility in combining a long-term professional career with the demands and uncertainties of public office. Elected office can thus be complementary, rather than antithetical, to the careers of many professionals, since political experience provides lawyers, businessmen and journalists with a range of useful contacts. Moreover, the high status of these occupations may favourably influence selectorates which choose party candidates.[12] For all these reasons, the limited number of women in these occupations means that they are at a clear numerical disadvantage in standing for office. As more women enter law, the media and business, however, more may climb the ladder leading to public office.

A further connection between employment and political participation is suggested by studies of campaign activism in the United States. Research has shown that female participation in politics is greatest among women working outside the home, since the latter develop greater political interest, competence and efficacy.[13] Work also offers women an organisational basis for political activity through trade unions and business groups. As more women enter the paid workforce, a greater number of motivated and well-connected female candidates may thus be willing to stand for public office.

DATA AND METHODS

In order to assess the relative impact of institutional, cultural and socio-economic factors upon female legislative representation, data from 24 developed liberal democracies (including 18 in Western Europe) were entered in a stepwise multiple regression analysis.[14] Each nation has been widely classified as a continuous or interrupted democracy on the basis of regular competitive elections, equal legal rights for women to participate as national legislative candidates, and developed economic systems.[15]

To measure institutional factors, countries were classified as either party-list proportional or majoritarian electoral systems (the latter included first-post-the-post, alternative vote, and single transferable vote systems).[16] To measure cultural factors, comparisons were made using a Political Egalitarianism index created from the 1977 Euro-barometer survey, which polled 8,791 respondents in the nine member states of the European Community.[17] Respondents were asked a series of four questions concerning their attitudes towards the role of women and men, from which an index measuring beliefs in political equality of the sexes in local, national and the European Parliaments was developed (see Table 2). While the Euro-barometer poll did not cover all 24 countries, it offers the most extensive cross-cultural data at present available. An alternative measure of cultural differences is also employed in this analysis, namely the strength of Catholicism versus Protestantism in the population, where we would expect Protestant cultures to be less traditional in the roles expected of women.[18] Lastly, to measure the impact of socio-economic variables, we included data

TABLE 2
POLITICAL EGALITARIANISM INDEX[a]

Positive Egalitarian Response (%)

	Belgium	Denmark	West Germany	France	Ireland	Italy	Luxem.	Neth.	United Kingdom
If there were more women on your local council would things go better or worse?	63	81	66	70	74	55	46	71	71
If there were distinctly more women in the National Parliament do you think things would go better or worse?	64	81	67	70	77	52	48	74	69
In general would you have more confidence in a man or a woman as your representative in Parliament?	53	71	52	61	46	49	42	63	52
For the European Parliament do you think it desirable or not that there should be quite a lot of women elected?	39	42	44	57	50	35	35	35	52
Average egalitarian score[b]	33	54	33	47	35	8	7	39	36

[a] N = 8791 respondents drawn from Euro-barometer survey, October/November, 1977

[b] score equals pro- minus anti-egalitarian responses

on the proportion of women in each country in the full-time paid workforce, and in specific occupations such as law, education and journalism.[19] To measure the influence of educational factors, the average proportion of women in the college population in each country over the last 30 years was included using UNESCO data.[20]

FINDINGS AND CONCLUSIONS

As reported in Table 3, regression results show that institutional factors related to the electoral system were most significant in shaping women's representation (beta = .65). Cultural attitudes as measured by the Egalitarianism Index were also significant, while the Catholic population and socio-economic factors were found to be insignificant. What are the explanations for, and implications of, this analysis?

TABLE 3
MULTIPLE REGRESSION ANALYSIS OF WOMEN IN NATIONAL LEGISLATIVE OFFICE, 1983[a]

Explanation	Independent Variable	Beta Coefficient
Institutional	Proportional Representation	.65[b]
Cultural	Egalitarianism index	.45[b]
	Catholic population (%)	.16
Socio-economic	Women in labour force (%)	.26
	Women as professionals (%)	.26
	Women in universities (%)	.14

[a] Number of cases = 24; MR = .82; r^r = .68
[b] Significance probably ≤ .05

The influence of electoral systems can be explained most clearly by comparing elections in the Netherlands, as an example of strict proportionality, with those in Britain, as a purely majoritarian system. In the former, voters chose between lists of party candidates within a single national constituency. Under this system, central party organisations have considerable influence over the nomination of candidates and, if they are committed to including more women, are able to do so. Parties may attempt to create a balanced ticket by including women and men, as well as all major regional, cultural, social and religious interests.[21] Moreover, in systems with preferential voting within PR, such as Norway, women's groups can manipulate party lists to their advantage by deleting men's names on an organised basis so that women rise to more favourable positions within the list.[22]

In majoritarian cases such as Britain, voters in a constituency chose a single candidate to represent them in Parliament. Under this system, there is relatively more emphasis upon individual candidates than parties. Since candidates' abilities, experience, policies, and personal characteristics are scrutinised, their sex may play a more important role than under PR arrangements. In addition, if central party organisations wanted to include more female candidates, they would find it relatively difficult to impose these wishes on local selection groups which frequently defend their independence in such matters. Quota systems to ensure a certain percentage of female candidates are therefore more difficult to implement in the plurality case.

The impact of institutional and specifically electoral arrangements upon female legislative participation may also be demonstrated within single systems. In France, for example, a notable disparity exists between the percentage of women in the National Assembly (4.3 per cent in 1979) and the French delegation to the EEC Parliament (21 per cent in 1979). In the former case, a two-ballot majority system in single-member constituencies is used, while for the European elections, France employs proportional representation within one national constituency.[23] The differences which voting systems produce in a simultaneous election can be seen most clearly in West Germany, where half of the Bundestag is selected by majoritarian single member districts and the rest by Land lists. As might be expected given our findings, the vast majority (80 per cent) of female members of the Bundestag enter by the latter route.[24]

In terms of cultural attitudes, we find that favourable attitudes towards female candidates are positively correlated with the number of women in office, but that electoral factors reflect a stronger association. We can thus conclude that a party-list proportional system of representation, combined with positive attitudes towards women in politics, are most likely to lead to gender parity in legislatures. The relative importance of these factors is clearly illustrated in the case of Switzerland, where women have greatly increased in national office under proportional representation despite the prevalence of traditional attitudes. That Switzerland is highly traditional in its attitudes can be shown in various ways. Switzerland was the last major European country to enfranchise women nationally, in 1971, when women were also permitted to stand for the Nationalrat and Standerat. Resistance to these changes continues, as reflected in 1982 when male citizens in one canton voted to deny women the vote in local elections.[25] Similarly, a recent cross-national Gallup poll reports that strong traditional attitudes persist; for example, one third of Swiss respondents believed that men should be breadwinners while women should remain in the home.[26] Despite the predominance of such conservative attitudes towards women's role, however, the first national election for which women could stand (1971) produced a level of five per cent female representation in the Nationalrat, increasing to 7.5 per cent in 1975 and 10.5 per cent in 1979. This level was twice the percentage obtained in a similar period in Britain as well as Canada and the USA, where there existed more favourable attitudes towards women in politics, a longer tradition of female participation and stronger women's movements pressing for political equality.

Finally, this analysis found that socio-economic factors, as measured by the percentage of women in the workforce, in the professions and in universities, were not significantly associated with the number of women in legislative office. That education and employment are relatively unimportant is shown more clearly in the North American than Western European cases, since in the former we find a relatively high proportion of women in universities and the paid labour force, yet comparatively few in national legislative office. This pattern suggests that even if women are making a breakthrough in such areas as private sector management, public administration, and the professions, which presumably provide strong qualifications and experience suitable for elective office, they will not necessarily make similar progress at the same time in politics. Given the many institutional barriers to political equality, including a resistance to the implementation of electoral reform in majoritarian systems, it seems unlikely that cross-national differences in the political position of women will diminish in the near future.

NOTES

1. The author thanks Jill Hills for suggestions on an earlier draft, and the University of Maine and Newcastle Polytechnic for facilitating the research project.
2. See R. D. Putnam, *The Comparative Study of Political Elites* (Englewood Cliffs, NJ: Prentice-Hall, 1976); and J. D. Aberbach, R. D. Putnam, and B. A. Rockman, *Bureaucrats and Politicians in Western Democracies* (Cambridge, MA: Harvard University Press, 1981).
3. See 'Women in European Parliament', supplement No. 4 to *Women of Europe* (Brussels: Commission of the European Communities, 1979); *Times Guide to the European Parliament* (London: Times of London, 1979); and *European Elections 1984: Results and Elected Members* (Brussels: EEC Directorate General for Information, 1984).
4. R. M. Kelly and M. Boutilier, *The Making of Political Women* (Chicago: Nelson Hall, 1978); and E. Vallance, *Women in the House* (London: Athlone, 1979).
5. See V. Bogdanor, *What is Proportional Representation?* (Oxford: Martin Robertson, 1984); F. Castles, 'Female Legislative Representation and the Electoral System', *Politics* 1 (1981), 21–27; M. Currell, *Political Woman* (London: Croom Helm, 1974); M. Duverger, *The Political Role of Women* (Paris: UNESCO, 1955); W. Kohn, *Women in National Legislatures* (New York: Praeger, 1980); W. R. Krauss, 'Political Implications of Gender Roles', *American Political Science Review* 68 (1974), 1906–23; J. Lovenduski and J. Hills (eds.), *The Politics of the Second Electorate* (London: Routledge 1981); I. N. Means, 'Political Recruitment of Women in Norway', *Western Political Quarterly* 25:3 (1972), 491–521; and W. Rule, 'How to Increase Feminist Representation in Parliament', paper presented at Second International Congress on Women, Groningen, 1984.
6. For further discussion of this problem, see J. Bochel and D. Denver, 'Candidate Selection in the Labour Party: What the Selectors Seek', *British Journal of Political Science* 13:1 (1983).
7. See Putnam, *Comparative Study*; J. Blondel, *Comparative Legislatures* (Englewood Cliffs, NJ: Prentice-Hall, 1973); and G. Loewenberg and S. C. Patterson, *Comparing Legislatures* (Boston: Little Brown, 1979).
8. Putnam, *Comparative Study*.
9. See S. Verba, *Modes of Democratic Participation* (Beverly Hills: Sage, 1971); G. A. Almond and S. Verba, *The Civic Culture* (Princeton: Princeton University Press, 1963); A. Inkeles, 'Participant Citizenship in Six Developing Countries', *American Political Science Review* 63 (1969); S. M. Lipset, *Political Man* (New York: Doubleday, 1960); and L. W. Milbrath, *Political Participation* (Chicago: Rand McNally, 1977).
10. Putnam, *Comparative Study*; and R. Davidson and W. J. Oleszek, *Congress and its*

Members (Washington, DC: Congressional Quarterly Press, 1981).
11. See Loewenberg and Patterson, *Comparing Legislatures*; and Blondel, *Comparative Legislatures*.
12. See M. L. Mezey, *Comparative Legislatures* (Durham, NC: Duke University Press, 1979).
13. See K. Andersen, 'Working Women and Political Participation', *American Journal of Political Science* 19:3 (1975) 439–53; and S. Welch, 'Women as Political Animals?' *American Journal of Political Science* 21:4 (1977), 711–30.
14. Stepwise multiple regression was selected in order to provide comparability with previous research, notably Rule, 'How to Increase', and W. Rule, 'Why Women Don't Run: The Critical Contextual Factors in Women's Legislative Recruitment', *Western Political Quarterly* 34:1 (1981), 60–77. Appropriate tests of tolerance were employed to check for multi-collinearity.
15. See D. A. Rustow, *A World of Nations* (Washington, DC: Brookings, 1967) and D. Butler, H. R. Penniman, and A. Ranney, *Democracy at the Polls* (Washington, DC: American Enterprise Institute, 1981).
16. Butler, Penniman, and Ranney.
17. The Euro-Barometer poll (August 1977) was conducted by a number of survey organisations in the nine member states on behalf of the EEC Directorate General for Information. See *Men and Women of Europe 1978* (Brussels: Commission of the European Communities, 1979).
18. This variable was measured as the percentage of Catholics versus Protestants in each national population, according to the *Europa Year Book* (London: Europa, 1983).
19. Data were drawn from *Yearbook of Labour Statistics* (Geneva: International Labour Organisation, 1983).
20. This category of higher education included women in universities, colleges, and technical training institutes, as reported in UNESCO Yearbooks between 1960 and 1980.
21. See V. Bogdanor, *The People and the Party System* (Cambridge: Cambridge University Press, 1981).
22. See T. Skard, 'Progress for Women', in C. F. Epstein and R. L. Coser (eds.), *Access to Power* (London: Allen & Unwin, 1981); and B. As, 'Norway: More Power to Women', paper presented at Second International Congress on Women, Groningen, 1984.
23. See V. Herman and M. Hagger, *The Legislation of Direct Elections to the European Parliament* (London: Gower, 1980).
24. See Kohn, *Women*.
25. See G. H. Flanz, *Comparative Women's Rights and Political Participation in Europe* (New York: Transnational, 1983).
26. See E. P. Hastings, *Index to International Public Opinion, 1978–79* (Westport, CT: Greenwood, 1980).